BARRIERS

By Ann Aschauer

"I was sure by now,
God, You would have reached down,
And wiped our tears away,
Stepped in and saved the day.
But once again, I say "Amen,"
And it's still raining . . ."

Casting Crowns

AF584735

978-1-60920-106-7
Printed in the United States of America

©2015 Ann Aschauer
All rights reserved

API
Ajoyin Publishing, Inc.
P.O. 342
Three Rivers, MI 49093
www.ajoyin.com

No part of this book may be reproduced or transmitted in any form or by any means, electronic or mechanical—including photocopying, recording, or by any information storage and retrieval system—without permission in writing from the publisher, except as provided by United States of America copyright law.

All scripture is NIV unless otherwise noted.

Please direct your inquiries to admin@ajoyin.com

Dedication

To the one God—Father, Jesus, Holy Spirit:

As I pray to the Father, through the Son, in the Spirit, You are still a mystery to me, a wondrous mystery I will never fully understand in this life. Thank You for Your patience with me while teaching me over the years about You, Your will, and Your kingdom.

Thank You for Your Word, the lamp to our feet and light to our path, and for the awesome power and privilege of prayer. Help us to pray according to Your will and to remove the barriers—those of the enemy and those of our own making. Help us to clear the way for You to be glorified in our lives, until we know You fully, even as we have been fully known.

To my husband Marty, so often the model of what Christ is like. Your love, provision, and protection enable me to do what I do. To my children, Joanna, Ben, and Kelly, thanks for letting me include you in my stories. (It isn't easy having a mom who writes and speaks.)

Thanks, Pastor Bruce, Tom, Tay, and Jordan, for letting me use your names. Thanks for the parts you've played in my story, along with people whose names I don't even know- a sky marshal, a Wyoming real estate agent, and others God has placed in my life at just the right time.

Thank you, Naghmeh Abedini and Nancy Sheldon, for letting me share your stories as well. You are truly inspirational women, and I am in awe of what the LORD is doing in and through you.

Tracy, Sharon, and Kelly, thanks for previewing the manuscript and encouraging me to go forward with this project. Pam, thanks for once again walking me through the process. Joe, thanks for your honest feedback. You helped me get my mind beyond the youth group and write like an adult! (Wow! How cool is that?! You are awesome, bro!)

To my Bible study sisters and prayer partners, thanks for your encouragement, your support, and most of all your faithfulness in praying for me. (After all, that's what this book is all about.)

Dedication

Contents

Prologue

Why tonight, of all nights?!

It was almost time for the big youth rally at our church. As one of the leaders I was anticipating a great outreach, and hoping and praying for a harvest of young souls. I had planned to be at the church early, but that night I had had to work later than expected. Now I had just enough time to swing by home and pick up my daughter Kelly, so I was driving through the pouring rain at the full 40 mph speed limit when it happened.

About a quarter mile from our house my eye caught a flash of black and white at my right headlight. It was only after I had heard the thud a split second later that it registered that a cat had darted in front of my minivan.

When I pulled into our driveway, Kelly was ready to go. She bounced down the front walk and hopped into the car with a cheery "Hi Mom!"

In contrast to her bubbly greeting, I merely stared ahead and grimly stated, "I just killed someone's cat."

"Oh no!" Kelly cried. "Was it Tux?"

Tux!

It had not even occurred to me that it might be the neighbors' cat that Kelly frequently cared for when they were out of town.

"I don't know," I moaned.

I slowed down as we passed the spot where the black and white heap of fur lay in the road, the cars passing over it every few seconds, but there was no way to tell if it was even a cat, much less the beloved pet that always appeared to be wearing a little tuxedo.

We arrived at the church right on time. I dropped Kelly off at the door and parked the car, but I couldn't bring myself to go inside until I found out whether or not the cat I had hit was the one that belonged to our neighbors. After an unsuccessful attempt to contact them by phone, I decided that even if it wasn't Tux, it was *someone*'s pet, and so for the sake of its owners I needed to get it out of the road before it got totally mutilated. So I made my way back to the scene of the crime.

I parked in the nearest driveway and took an old sheet and a box out of the back of the car and prepared to scoop up the remains. When there was a break in the traffic, I approached the mound of fur.

To my horror, it lifted its head and looked at me!

It's still alive?!

I took another step closer, and the light of the streetlamp reflected off a tag that said "Tux."

Dang!

"Oh, Tux, baby, I am *so sorry*!" As I gingerly scooped him up into the sheet, he let out a predictable "Meow!" of pain, and I noticed a small trickle of blood coming from his mouth.

I won't bore you with the details of the next hour, but here's the Reader's Digest version: I tried to find the neighbors, set off their burglar alarm, talked to the friendly neighborhood police, tried the neighbors' cell phone, tried my husband's cell phone, and explained to the after-hours vet that even if I could drive the forty minutes to the animal ER, I didn't feel I had the right to have someone else's cat euthanized without their knowledge or permission. Finally, I set the box down in our foyer, as our dog, Mr. Hollywood, was going crazy on the other side of the kitchen door. Tux was looking at me sadly, the trickle of blood drying on his little chin, and I finally did what I should have done in the first place; I decided to pray. (You would think someone who had been fasting and praying all day would have come up with this idea sooner.) I laid my hands on Tux's little head and said "Lord, please, either heal him or let him die. Don't make him suffer any more." Not knowing what else to say, I closed my eyes and sang a couple of verses of "Jesus Loves Me."

Moments later I heard a "*Meow*!" I opened my eyes and looked at the box. It was empty, and Tux was walking around my house, complaining! I was overjoyed for a moment but then realized the youth rally was starting in five minutes.

"I don't have time for this!" I muttered. Grabbing the cat, I stuck him in the bathroom, closed the door, and headed for church.

The evening was wonderful! Kids came forward at the altar call, and I got to pray with a couple of them for the Lord to come into their lives and transform them.—And I had almost missed it because of a cat!

I came home to find my husband Marty in the foyer talking to the neighbors, who were holding Tux, who was perfectly fine and lived for years after that.

OK, I really told you that story so I could tell you this one . . .

A couple of days after the Tux incident, I came home to a scene that was all too familiar. The house was quiet, and my darling daughter was in the den with the lights off, the curtains drawn, and the door shut. I knew immediately that she was in the throes of a full-blown migraine.

I hated them. She had suffered from these monster headaches since at the age of four she would lie on the couch crying, "My head hurts!" We had been to doctors, specialists, chiropractors, nutritionists, allergists, orthodontists, and even a surgeon, and of course, Kelly had had a *lot* of prayer. But remembering the recent miracle of the resurrected cat, I believed the prayer route was worth one more try, so I quietly went into the den, where she lay on the couch, softly crying.

"Hi, sweetie," I whispered. "Would you like me to pray for you?" Without opening her eyes she nodded. I gently laid my hands on her, trying to remember how I had done it the other night when I'd prayed for Tux.

"*Please*, Lord . . . *please* heal my daughter!" It was all I had left. I knew her healing would not come from my words but from the power of the Divine Physician, so I waited. And what happened next was . . .

Absolutely nothing.

And I was *angry.*

I tiptoed out of the room and quietly closed the door before letting the rage out.

"*LORD?!*"(It amazes me how I can call Him "Lord" and at the same time be shaking my fist at Him.) "*Someday* You and I are going to meet face to face, and *SOMEDAY* You're going to explain to me why I can say *ONE prayer* for a *STUPID CAT*, You *resurrect* it, and I've been praying for my daughter for *twelve years*, and I've s-seen *n-nothing!*" By this time I was crying harder than Kelly was, and although I no doubt deserved a lightning bolt to the head for the way I was speaking to the Almighty; He understood I was hurting, and I could sense His big arms around me.

When God speaks to you, you just know it. It doesn't have to be an audible voice or writing in the sky, you just sense it in your heart. (The better we know Him, the more clearly He speaks.) At that point the Lord waited a moment for me to calm down. Then He spoke to me, silently but very clearly, the last thing I expected to hear from Him:

You don't have to wait that long, I'll explain it now.

Huh? I stood frozen in place, kind of the way one stands when getting a precarious cell phone connection for fear of losing it.

OK . . . I'm listening . . .

Introduction

This book is for anyone who has ever wondered why we so often see immediate answers to the spontaneous little prayers for a parking spot, a lost shoe, or something equally trivial, and yet see no results when praying about the really important things. It seems each of us has at least one concern that has been prayed over for days, weeks, even years, with little or no perceived progress.

This book is also for anyone who has asked, "How come *they* get all the miracles?" We hear about miraculous answers to prayer, usually in Third World countries—healings, deliverance, amputated limbs growing back, even people's being raised from the dead—and wonder, *Why don't we see these kinds of miracles here? Shouldn't answered prayer—even miracles—be a normal occurrence for a Christian?* Reading the book of Acts, one would think so. Is there something about our present-day culture, in this allegedly "Christian nation" that actually *interferes* with this kind of "miracles-every-day" Christianity? Is there something wrong within *us* who are praying that is keeping God from moving in our lives the way He wants to—the way He *longs* to?

I have found that the Bible has much to say about why so many of our prayers seem to go unanswered, and most of what I have learned pertains to barriers to prayer that we can actually do something about.

I don't claim to know everything about prayer; much of it is still a mystery to me. But what I do know—including what the Lord spoke to me that one frustrating night—I want to share with anyone who desires to see God's hand at work more in his or her life. Although I'm guessing that we will never in this life understand everything about how prayer works, we can know that our heavenly Father does want us to pray! And in the meantime, the Bible has much to say about hindrances to prayer that we can learn from and apply to our lives—*if* we're willing to submit to Him and make the changes in mindset and attitude that He requires. Then, once we are "on the same page" with Him, we will be astounded as we watch Him do more than we can ask or even imagine! (Ephesians 3:20).

Miracles are not just for ancient times. If God is "the same, yesterday, today, and forever," (Hebrews 13:8) He is doing great things *now*. If you are serious about doing your part in His Kingdom, this book offers some possible solutions from God's Word for the roadblocks you are experiencing in your prayer life. While we don't understand everything, we should act on what we do know, which God has made very clear.

Then, even when we have reached the end of our understanding, we have a perfect opportunity to exercise the faith that He loves until the day it is all explained to us.

Chapter One

BARRIER #1

LACK OF RELATIONSHIP

"I know my sheep, and my sheep know me."
John 10:14

"Excuse Me, Do I Know You?"

I've heard many an atheist declare that God doesn't answer prayer, because there is no God. I often get the feeling it's not that this person doesn't believe in God but that he's mad at Him for some reason. I also get the feeling that this person is mad at God for not doing something for him that he wanted, or for letting something happen to him that he *didn't* want. But if this person doesn't acknowledge God's existence, doesn't love God, and has no desire to know Him, does God owe him anything? Or has the modern American "entitlement" mentality spilled over into our spiritual lives?

But what if you *do* believe in God?

James puts it bluntly: "You believe that there is one God. Good! Even the demons believe that—and shudder!" (James 2:19) Sadly, it is possible to believe in God and yet not *know* or *love* Him.

In other words, it is possible to believe in God without having a *relationship* with Him. Think about it: You can believe in George Washington without ever having met him, to know *of* him without truly *knowing* him. There is more to knowing someone than merely believing that he or she exists, and there is more to being a true Christian than just believing in Christ.

Jesus Himself said that on the Day of Judgment He would say to many, "I never knew you." (Matthew 7:23) I think those would be the saddest, most horrifying words I could ever hear. And I believe that they will be sad words for our Savior as well, because He *wants* to know us—He wants *us* to know *Him*, to have an intimate relationship with Him, not just say we believe in Him so we can ask for stuff.

This relationship with Jesus takes place on a number of levels. He is, among other things, our Creator (John 1:1–3), our King (Revelation 11:15), our Savior (John 3:16–18), our Prince of Peace (Isaiah 9:6), our Counselor (Isaiah 9:6), our Friend (John 15:13–15), our Shepherd (John 10:11), our Father (Isaiah 9:6), our Bridegroom (Revelation 19:7).

Face it, He's our everything! But would anyone know that by the way we treat Him?

Gift or Giver?

The speaker at the youth retreat gave some vivid illustrations as he encouraged the students to draw close to the Lord in a personal relationship, but to me the most poignant was the story of the little girl planning her birthday party.

The child's father was quite wealthy and could give his daughter pretty much anything she wanted for her party. Part of their birthday tradition was to plan the party together, and every year it was a special "Daddy-daughter" time.

This year the little girl wanted ponies at her party—lots and lots of ponies. The father could easily afford to get as many ponies as he wanted for his daughter's party, but there was one little problem: Daddy was allergic to ponies.

"Honey, I'm not sure we can do ponies."

"But I WANT PONIES!" the child demanded.

"Honey, Daddy's allergic to ponies." Seeing that the little girl didn't quite understand, he continued, "If we had ponies at your party, Daddy couldn't come."

The child responded, "Then I don't want you to come."

At this point in the story a cry of sheer pain came from several girls in the audience, immediately sensing how deeply such a statement would wound a loving father. The speaker paused, and then asked the question of the day.

"But how many of *us* do that to our *heavenly* Father?"

The speaker paused, and the room became very quiet.

"How many of us have the attitude: 'God, thanks for all the stuff. I really like it when You bless me. Keep those blessings coming! But . . . a relationship with You? Spending time with You? . . . eh . . . I don't think I'm interested in *that.*'"

It has been said, "A little knowledge is a dangerous thing." For me the operative word is "little." In the Sermon on the Mount Jesus said,

> Which of you, if his son asks for bread, will give him a stone? Or if he asks for a fish, will give him a snake? If you, then, though you are evil, know how to give good gifts to your children, how much more will your Father in heaven give good gifts to those who ask him?
>
> Matthew 7:9–11

At first glance, it might seem as though Jesus is saying the Father gives good stuff to anyone who asks Him. But notice that the context is a *father* giving to *his children*. I'm guessing you don't routinely give good gifts away to children you don't know. But if you have children of your own, you know that most parents will do or give anything for the sake of a child.

Oddly, in the same paragraph, in the very next verse Jesus says, "So in everything, do to others what you would have them do to you, for this sums up the Law and the Prophets." (vs. 12) You probably recognize this as the "Golden Rule," but what does the Golden Rule have to do with asking and receiving? Could it be that the person who treats others this way is *showing* that he is a child of God, because in loving others he's resembling his Father? Jesus seems to be implying that if we treat others the way we want to be treated, we should have no hesitation about asking our Father for "good gifts."

But how many Christians consistently live this kind of godly lifestyle?

Foul Weather Children

Many of us know what it feels like to have a friend or relative that we see only when he wants something. If we don't like that kind of treatment, why would we expect God to put up with it? There are plenty of individuals who give no thought to God or what He wants, never spend time with Him, never read His Word, never worship Him, and never show love to others, other than perfunctory politeness. And yet when trouble hits, that person goes running to God crying for help. Now God is gracious, and He *may* in His mercy send help, but He owes that person nothing. He has every right to say "Excuse Me, do I know you?"

The demons understand this principle, better than many Christians.

> Some Jews who went around driving out evil spirits tried to invoke the name of the Lord Jesus over those who were demon possessed. They would say, "In the name of Jesus, whom Paul preaches, I command you to come out." Seven sons of Sciva, a Jewish priest, were doing this. [One day] the evil spirit answered them, "Jesus I know, and I know about Paul, but who are you?" Then the man who had the evil spirit jumped on them and overpowered them all. He gave them such a beating that they ran out of the house naked and bleeding."
>
> Acts 19:13–16

By What Authority?

The name of Jesus is *not* a magic word, to be used by anyone who wants to get something from God. God is *not* a genie in a bottle! In Middle Eastern folklore a genie (or jinni) was a being that had the power to travel places in the blink of an eye and make palaces materialize. And yet this powerful being could be possessed and commanded by a mere mortal. It amazes me that such a concept was ever taken seriously. We may *wish* we had authority over that kind of power, but that's not how real life works.

Write this down: **The One with the power has the authority**. (Keep in mind, He also has the wisdom. What we think we want could very well be disastrous if we were to get it!)

If you're reading this book to learn some formula to get God to give you more stuff, you're reading it for the wrong reason. Please know that God delights in blessing His children, but know, too, that the greatest blessing of all is *being His child.*

The Most Intimate Relationship

But there is even more to a relationship with God than the privilege of being His child. As Christians, we get to be the *Bride* of Christ!

The Bible is filled with imagery involving the Lord and His Bride, some of it not so positive.

When Israel neglected the Lord, wandered away from Him, even turned to other gods, it broke His heart. Most of the book of Hosea consists of God's pouring out His heartache over His unfaithful bride. The apostate Church is referred to as a "harlot."

At the same time, Scripture is filled with beautiful sentiments of the love of the Bridegroom for His Bride. The love song known as the Song of Solomon is about the gloriously intimate relationship between a husband and wife and is often equated with the Lord's relationship with Israel.

In the New Testament the Church is referred to as "the Bride of Christ." In fact, in the book of Revelation the description of Jesus being reunited with His Church depicts a marriage feast!

> Let us rejoice and be glad
> And give him glory!
> For the wedding of the Lamb [Jesus] has come,
> And his bride has made herself ready.
>
> Revelation 19:7

What is our relationship with our Bridegroom like? And what can a bride of Christ expect from her husband?

In the book of Esther, the Jews were in danger of extinction. God raised up a young Jewish girl, Hadassah, or Esther, to be in a position to save her people. Out of all the young maidens in the kingdom of Persia, Esther was the one who pleased King Xerxes, and he made her his bride.

At the crucial point in the story, when the fate of the Jewish people was on the line, Esther approached the King. His response when he saw her: "What is it, Queen Esther? What is your request? Even up to half the kingdom, it shall be given you." (Esther 5:3)

Now if that was the response of a pagan king to the wife who pleased him, would it make sense to expect any less of the God of the universe, who has loved us to the point of death, and who has authority over everything?

> He who did not spare his own Son, but gave him up for us all—how will he not also, along with him, graciously give us all things?
>
> Romans 8:32

What kind of Bride are we? The one that grieves the heart of the Bridegroom with neglect and unfaithfulness? Or the Bride that He delights in—the Bride that *delights herself in Him* as well?

In Perfect Unity

The 17th chapter of John has the longest recorded prayer that Jesus prayed. This could well have been His most important prayer, because He knew He was about to be arrested and killed.

If you know you're about to die, you're going to skip the small talk and get right to what's most important, so this prayer gives us valuable insight about what was closest to Jesus' heart during His final hours.

First He prayed for Himself, for strength to carry out the task before Him. Then He prayed for His disciples who were with Him.

Finally, He prayed for *us!*

> "My prayer is not for them [the disciples] alone. I pray also for those who will believe in me through their message, that all of them may be one, Father, just as you are in me and I am in you. May they also be in us so that the world may believe that you have sent me. I have given them the glory that you gave me, that they may be one as we are one: I in them and you in me. May they be brought to complete unity to let the world know that you sent me and have loved them even as you have loved me.

"Father, I want those you have given me to be with me where I am, and to see my glory, the glory you have given me because you loved me before the creation of the world."

John 17:20–26

Notice, Jesus didn't say one word about our getting everything right, performing miracles, or even our succeeding all the time. However, He did mention that He wants us to be one with Him. And He wants us to be one with the Father: "that they also may be in us," "that they may be one: I in them and you in me." "I want those you have given me to be with me where I am." ". . . and that I myself may be in them."

Confused?

I'm a visual type, so to help myself picture what this looks like, I use a small card and three different sized envelopes as an illustration. (You might want to do this yourself and keep it in your Bible as a reminder.) Starting with the card, write "Jesus" on one side and "the Father" on the other, since Jesus and His Father are one. Put that card in the smallest of the three envelopes . . . Now if you have asked Jesus to be your Savior, write your name on that envelope, because He's in you, and since He and His Father are one, the Father is in you, too!

Now take the envelope with your name on it and put it in the next smallest envelope, and write "Son" on it, because if the Son of God is in you, you are in Him . . .

Now since the Son is in the Father, put it all in the last envelope and mark it "Father." This is how we are one with the Father and the Son. (The Holy Spirit's in there, too, but we'll leave that for another time.)

So, what happens when the world and/or the devil come to attack you? Well, in order to get to you, first they have to go through the Father, then through the Son, and when they finally get to you . . . they find you full of Jesus and His Father! So really, what do we have to be afraid of?

That intimacy—being one with the Lord—is the greatest security we could ever hope for.

"You have not, because you ask not."

James 4:2c

Let's admit it, sometimes we don't get answers to prayer simply because we don't pray. Why do we fail to pray?

Maybe deep down we don't really think prayer would do any good. (That barrier of doubt will be dealt with in another chapter.)

It's a vicious cycle:

1. We start slacking off and fail to nurture our relationship with God by spending time with Him *daily*, and so
2. We get out of the *habit* of praying about anything and everything.
3. That lack of daily communication actually contributes to other problems, including the problem of doubt: Because we aren't in touch with God, we don't know Him.
4. Not knowing Him, we doubt prayer will work, because we haven't *seen* prayer work, because we *haven't prayed!*

There's only one way to stop this kind of downward spiral—*reverse it.* There are four steps to that dance, too: pray, watch, give thanks, and share. It's not complicated. In fact, it makes all the sense in the world.

1. People who have prayers answered are people who *pray* and *expect* God to answer.
2. Because they expect God to answer, they're *watching* for the answer. Because they're watching for the answer, when it comes, they *see* it—even the unexpected, "not-what-I-asked-for-but-even-better" answers.
3. When they see the answer, they *rejoice,* and they *thank God.*
4. Then they share their good news with others. (After praying, seeing the answer, rejoicing, and thanking God, it would be hard *not* to tell someone else!)

Then as they share these experiences with others, their faith is reinforced.

With their faith reinforced, they're encouraged to pray some more. (And we're back to step 1.)

This may sound like grass-roots simplicity, but to be successful in prayer, one needs to *pray.* A good place to start is asking God to *help* you pray, and ask Him to help you recognize the answers when He sends them. When unexpected things come up—or even unexpected thoughts, instead of feeling derailed in your prayers, just continue praying for whatever you're going through at the time. (I did that once and saw a cat resurrected!) And whatever happens, remember to thank Him for the answers. Grateful people are happy people. Happy people tend to share good things with others. And as you share your good news, not only do *they* hear what you're saying, *you*'re hearing *yourself* tell the story, too! Just watch what this does for your faith, and for your relationship with the Lord.

Sometimes

When we first moved to southeastern Michigan, I attended a small church where a number of my friends belonged. The people were friendly, kind, and sincere, and I attended for almost a year before the pastor approached me about becoming a full-fledged member. He gave me a pamphlet explaining the denomination's doctrine and "special rules," and I told him I would prayerfully consider it.

The doctrines, for the most part, seemed pretty biblically sound, but as I already knew, the denomination had its own rules that distinguished it from most evangelical churches, rules against going to movies, joining clubs, dancing, and a few minor things that weren't part of my life anyway.

I sincerely wanted to be where God wanted me, and although I enjoyed movies and dancing, and my parents had belonged to a country club when I was growing up, I was perfectly willing to give up those things—*if* God was asking me to. The reason I was devoting some time and prayer to the issue was that I wanted to be sure it was *God* telling me, not men. I had my own opinion of those things, but I knew enough to know that my opinion was no more valuable than anyone else's; the only opinion that mattered was God's. So I remained secluded for a few days, speaking about these rules to no one except God, and reading no literature about it except the Bible.

After three days, I was as confused as ever. Closing my Bible in frustration, I blurted out, "God, *just tell me!* Is it wrong to dance?" I sat listening for that still, small voice, and somewhat to my surprise, I heard it in my heart and mind.

Sometimes.

"Well, is it wrong to go to movies?"

Sometimes.

"Is it wrong to belong to a club?"

Sometimes. I "heard" it clearly, but I wasn't sure it was helping.

"But that means I'm going to have to pray about everything I do!"

That's right!

Suddenly it made sense to me. As a conscientious, somewhat self-righteous Christian, prone to the occasional guilt trip, I wanted a clear list of do's and don'ts that I could follow and *know* I was doing the right thing. But God desired something higher than that for me. He wanted a *relationship* with me! If I had clear-cut rules, it would be too easy to just run on "automatic," and even if I were doing the "right" things—and refraining from doing the "wrong" things—all the time, I could forget my dependence on God and possibly drift away from Him without even realizing it.

But the Lord would rather have me close to Him, "praying without ceasing," and taking each situation moment by moment, even if it meant I'd sometimes make mistakes.

Hmm . . .

Maybe you've read this far and have come to realize that you don't *have* a faith to speak of—no relationship with the Lord at all. Maybe you used to go to church—maybe you go to church now, but you're realizing that going to church doesn't make you a child of God, any more than walking into someone's home makes you a member of his family.

Jesus told Nicodemus "No one can see the kingdom of God unless he is born again." (John 3:3) Earlier on in that gospel John states,

> "Yet to all who received him, to those who believed in his name, he gave the right to become children of God—children born not of natural descent, nor of human decision or a husband's will, but born of God."
>
> John 1:12–13

How does one "receive" Jesus? It goes beyond belief. It's one thing to hear a knocking, look through the peephole and say, "Yep, that's Jesus." It's quite another to open the door and invite Him in.

Please don't misunderstand. Believing is a good place to start. It *is* important to understand and believe the gospel, so here's my version in a nutshell:

If we are to believe the "good news," we need to understand the bad news—that "all have sinned and fallen short of the glory of God," (Romans 3:23) and "the wages of sin is death." (Romans 6:23) According to these verses, we are all under an eternal death sentence. But Jesus paid the penalty for our sins on the Cross to give eternal life to whoever believes in Him. That's the good news. In fact, that's the best news anyone could ever hear!

If we truly believed that Jesus paid for our sins and we're off the hook, would we just think >*Whew!*< *That's a relief!*—and go on our merry way without giving it another thought? If that's the way we treat our Savior, do we *really* believe He died for us? Knowing that someone wonderful loves me enough to be willing to die to save me from certain death (not to mention hell!) and that He's alive and making Himself available to have a relationship with me, I'd be crazy not to want it!

So maybe for you it's time to *really* believe—to realize just how much Jesus has done for you, and then take the next step, from *believing* in Jesus to *receiving* Him. The exact words you pray aren't important; He knows your intentions. Just open up your heart and tell Him you want Him in your life. Repent—that is, acknowledge your sins and be willing to turn away from them. Decide that from now on you will let Him direct you in the way *He* wants you to go, and trust that His plan for you is the best. In other words, you've accepted Him as *Savior*, now make Him your *Lord.*

If you've just made that decision—Welcome to the family!

Chapter Two

BARRIER

#2

MISDIRECTED ATTENTION

"The seed that fell among thorns stands for those who hear, but as they go on their way they are choked by life's worries, riches and pleasures, and they do not mature."

Luke 8:14

What are you looking at?

Psalm 37:4 says, "Delight yourself in the Lord, and he will give you the desires of your heart." I happen to think this is one of the most misunderstood verses of Scripture.

The standard interpretation of this verse seems to be that if you pray to God and really believe, He'll give you whatever you want.

Really?

I think this kind of reasoning reflects the selfish mindset of many believers today. We want what we want, so what do we have to do to get it? In other words, how do I butter up God enough to get Him to give me that house in Maui?

But it doesn't say "butter up," it says, "*Delight* yourself in the *Lord*." Doesn't that mean *He* is my *true* source of joy? And it doesn't say, "He'll give you what you desire," it says, "He will give you the desires of your heart." Could that mean that first He gives us the desires themselves, and *then* fulfills them?

I've found that if I delight in Him, giving Him everything I have and everything I am, He changes *me*. Often this means He changes my desires. Then as my heart is aligned to His, His desires become mine. Now as I pray for what I truly desire, I'm praying *His will.* And that's when I start seeing Him answer!

I've heard that the original word translated "delight" means literally "to set before oneself" It's like a man who sets a picture of his wife and child on his desk at work, where he can easily see it. Looking at it makes him happy, because he loves them—is delighted with them. When we go to God early in the day, we mentally "set Him before us," focusing on Him. Too many times we get it backwards. We focus on what we want. We make our plans. Then like good Christian people, we ask God to bless our plans. And later we ask in frustration, "Why didn't You bless our plans?"

I can see the answer to that question illustrated every morning at our house.

Mr. Hollywood is a "morning dog." This little guy *loves* breakfast time, because he gets his food, fun, and exercise all at the same time. Every morning I sit with his bowl at the top of our winding stairs and randomly send each morsel of dog chow up one hall or the other, down to the landing, or all the way to the first floor. Our little guy gets quite a workout chasing down each piece. I try to mix it up, so he's not just running the same pattern all the time. Usually in his excitement he gets ahead of the game and runs to where he *thinks* the next treat is going. He'll stand there, poised, waiting, while I throw the piece somewhere else. This has been going on ever since we started playing this game a couple of years ago, and every day I think, *When is he going to figure out he's got to watch me? I mean, I realize he's is not the brightest bulb on the tree, but seriously, how long is it going to take him to learn this simple lesson?!*

Well . . . How long is it going to take *us*? How many of us are running at top speed to where *we think* the blessings are, only to be disappointed?

I have a radical proposal. What if we spent time at the beginning of each day delighting ourselves in our Creator—worshiping, reading His word, talking to Him, *listening* to Him? What do you think would happen if we stopped second-guessing God and just let Him take us where *He* wants us to go?

There's only one way to find out.

A Mary, or a Martha?

Maybe you're *not* one of those Christians I just described, who are just in it for the blessings. Maybe you truly want to please God and be a blessing to others, and the way you do that is by "going about doing good." I've been there, and it makes sense. After all, Jesus said, "If you love Me, you will obey what I command," (John 14:15) and for some of us it comes naturally to express our love by serving, working, *doing*.

In the gospel of Luke, Martha was such a person. She and her sister Mary and brother Lazarus frequently opened up their home to Jesus and His disciples. From what we read in the gospels, Jesus must have felt at home there; obviously, Martha had the gift of hospitality.

We have to appreciate what it was like to host Jesus, accompanied by twelve disciples and, for all we know, numerous other followers. With no deep freezers or microwaves, preparing a meal for this crew must have been quite an undertaking, and on one occasion, described in Luke 10:38–42, we know Martha was feeling pressured. (The NIV uses the word "distracted.") Luke describes the moment she snapped.

With meal preparation in full swing, Martha spotted her sister Mary, sitting serenely at the feet of Jesus. Her reaction must have been the First Century equivalent of "*Are you kidding me?!*" Any stressed out hostess would have reacted the same way.

Martha was so outraged she actually interrupted Jesus' teaching to demand, "Tell her to help me!" (Luke 10:40)

Jesus, however, neither justified Martha nor stressed over her situation.

> "Martha, Martha," the Lord answered, "you are worried and upset about many things, but only one thing is needed. Mary has chosen what is better, and it will not be taken away from her."
>
> Luke 10:42

We aren't told how Martha responded. I hope she took the hint and sat down with her sister, but whether or not she did, Jesus had made His priorities crystal clear. Serving is good; relationship is better. Besides, neglecting relationship for the sake of serving can bring one dangerously close to the belief (conscious or not) that we are, at least partly, saving ourselves through our dedication to good works. But as I hope has been made clear in Chapter One, we are saved because of what *Jesus* has done for *us*, not the other way around. Acts of service are an outgrowth of the love relationship we have with Him.

Serving. Relationship. We can (and should) have both! But serving *begins* with relationship. It's a matter of **focus**. Martha was focused on doing things *for* Jesus; Mary was focused on *Jesus*. All you Martha's out there, consider this: If Jesus' throat got dry from teaching and He wanted a cup of water, whom would He have asked? It wasn't Martha. Jesus would have had to (a) find out where she was and (b) flag her down to let her know what He wanted her to do.

No, I'm guessing He would have asked the one who appeared to be "doing nothing," who was making herself available to serve Him at any given moment.

Yes, serve the Lord in whatever way He is calling you to serve Him. But in order to know what that is, it's necessary to spend time at His feet. In other words, in order to truly "wait on Him," one must, quite literally, *wait* on Him.

We Americans aren't used to waiting. With our drive-up windows, instant messaging, and a hundred other ways to speed up our already rushed lives, we rarely sit and pray, ponder, or meditate. And when we do, we feel guilty for "not getting anything done!"

Even if we don't feel guilty, there are those Martha-types who may be critical of the Mary-types who enjoy fellowship with Jesus when there is *so much that needs to be done!* Occasionally someone may point out their obvious exhaustion from *over*doing, but I have heard more than one Martha respond by declaring self-righteously, "I'd rather burn out than rust out!"

I have learned that whether you burn out or rust out, you're still *out.*

During one of my many seasons of "Martha-ism," as I was complaining of exhaustion—between Bible studies, youth groups, hospital volunteer work, and, oh yes, raising children—a friend seemed at first to be offering me some encouragement by saying, "You know, if you were to do just a *little* more . . ." (I perked up awaiting the next assignment of something I "ought to" be doing.) ". . . if you were to spread yourself just a *little* thinner, . . . you just might reach the point of complete ineffectiveness!"

It took me only a moment to realize that the enthusiasm in my friend's voice was pure sarcasm. Message received.

Rushing from one religious activity to another can leave us frazzled, grouchy, irritable, and *ineffective.* We can find ourselves doing "good" things for the wrong reasons, not to please God but to impress one another with our own importance. By cramming as many activities as possible into our schedules in an effort to try to be "all things to all people," we can end up not only with way too much on our plates, but resenting others for not helping us with the overload of projects we've put on *ourselves*! This is *not* the way to "serve the Lord with gladness!" (Please don't ask me how I know this.) It's also an implied denial of the gospel—the Good News—that we are saved by *faith.*

One Thing

"One thing I ask of the Lord, this is what I seek."

Psalm 27:4

The 1980's movie "City Slickers" was not exactly a Christian movie, and Curly, the quiet, macho cowboy the men looked up to, wasn't exactly a preacher, but toward the end of the film he made a profound point. When one of the "city slickers" that had come out west to find himself, asked what the secret to life was, Curly replied that it was "one thing." When the city slicker asked him what that one thing was, Curly told him, "That's what you've got to figure out." The young man was frustrated by that non-answer, but in the end he finally realized that what the cowboy was saying was that life has meaning only when it is dedicated to *one thing*, not a plethora of unrelated goals and random pursuits. That one thing will be different for each person.

Of course, for the Christian that one purpose should always be to please God, but once we have placed our faith in Him, each of us will have our own unique way of fulfilling God's call on our lives. No one else can tell us what our calling is, and no one else can do what we are called to do.

It's time to stop being distracted by everybody else's ideas of what we "ought to" be doing; there's no way we'll accomplish everything the world says we need to accomplish, anyway. It's time to sit at the feet of Jesus, listen with our hearts, and ask Him, "Lord, what do *You* want?" That's really all that matters.

"Lord, what do You want me to do?"

I asked the Lord that question soon after our youngest child left for college. I was retired from teaching, and my husband was in the process of retiring. It was beginning to look as though we'd have all that time we had always wanted to pursue new things, but I knew myself well enough to know that if I just hit the floor running, I'd soon have a schedule crammed full of stuff, perhaps none of which was what I *should* be doing. So I asked . . .

I fell asleep asking, "Lord, what do You want me to do next?" and I'm afraid the emphasis was on the word "do." But I woke up the next morning with a beautiful song playing in my head. Although it wasn't a hymn or worship song, I believe it was God's speaking to my heart. It was one of the gorgeous melodies from "Phantom of the Opera," and as for the lyrics, I only knew the last line of the song:

Love me, that's all I ask of you.

I remembered my question of the night before and thought—*Seriously?! That's it?* It seemed too simple.

But as I submitted to that request, giving the Lord all my love and attention, I found I could "hear" His voice more clearly, feel His presence more sweetly.

It wasn't that He wanted me to spend the rest of my life sitting at His feet, ignoring everything and everybody else. But it was, for that moment, what He wanted me to do. It was the starting point for anything and everything else He wanted to do in my life. In the months that followed, from that position of sheer love and adoration, I have been led into various ways to serve Him. The difference is, I don't have to feel frustrated or guilty at the slow pace at which things seem to be going. Better slowly in the right direction than running full speed down some rabbit trail of my own making. Not that I don't occasionally feel frustrated or guilty, but I don't *have to*. There are still times the Martha in me shows up, and I have to make a conscious effort to stop, take a deep breath, and go back to Jesus. I need to ask myself, "Do I want to wear myself out doing a hundred things God hasn't asked me to do, or would I rather do the one thing He *is* asking me to do—and do it well?"

This may sound unrealistic and impossible to live out if you're a Martha-type, but trust me, it can be done . . . eventually. God is patient. And anyway, with Him *all* things are possible.

"Are you forgetting something?"

There's another reason we can get stressed out, even doing the right things. I remember so well a "teachable moment" I experienced many years ago during the height of my "Martha" season.

As I collapsed into bed the night before Thanksgiving. I honestly thought I was going to be able to stay there for a while. I had been up and busy non-stop for the past eighteen hours, cleaning the house, making the beds for my in-laws, shopping for food, and preparing as much of the Thanksgiving feast as I could ahead of time. Exhausted, I figured I was overdue for a good rest.

Silly me.

"Mommy, I don't feel good." I opened one eye and saw a sad-looking little girl. *Poor Joanna*, I thought. I had fixed up my daughter's room for the in-laws, and she had been relegated to the couch in the den. I suspected that she "wasn't feeling good" because she was trying to sleep in a strange place, and I figured it wouldn't hurt to let her sleep one night in her own bed before Grandma and Grampa came. I figured it was no big deal. She'd had a bath and her pajamas were clean. I would just put fresh pillowcases on the pillows the next day, and we'd be all set. I took her back to her own room, tucked her in, gave her a kiss, and staggered back to my own bed, ready for a "long winter's nap."

Silly me.

After a tantalizing fifteen minutes of slumber, I awoke to the unmistakable sound of a small child with stomach flu. I stumbled into her room just in time to see the child, the pajamas, the bedding, the bedroom carpet, and the bathroom rug covered in the evidence.

Back to Square One.

Moving like a zombie, I filled the tub, stripped the bed, started the washer, bathed Joanna and shampooed her hair, got her into clean pajamas, remade the bed and tucked her back in.

She fell back asleep instantly, and I envied her. I still had to clean the bathroom and try to get the stains and stench out of the carpet.

As I worked into the wee hours of the morning, I began to be aware of a growing resentment eating at me, and as Thanksgiving morning approached, thankfulness was the furthest thing from my mind. My husband, who had slept peacefully through the whole episode, happily slept on, and somehow I felt the whole thing was *so unfair. How dare he sleep!* After all, it was *his* parents who were coming, and I'd knocked myself out trying to make everything nice for them . . .! (And I continued with a string of equally ridiculous rants.)

I guess Someone finally decided He had heard enough silliness from me. As I scrubbed the carpet furiously, the "still, small voice" of God (or maybe it was just plain common sense) spoke distinctly to me:

Why don't you ask him to help you?

"Marty! Would you *please* come help me here?!" My tone wasn't exactly sweet, but my dear husband, rudely awakened from a deep sleep, roused himself with a groggy but agreeable "Oh! . . . Sure!" He staggered into the bathroom, grabbed another rag, and then my husband—a PhD with degrees in chemical engineering, environmental engineering, and civil engineering—knelt beside me and helped blot the vomit out of the carpet.

Silly me.

Seriously. I felt *very* silly—resenting him for not doing what I hadn't yet *asked* him to do.

And as Thanksgiving dawned, I did feel grateful.

James says "You do not have, because you do not ask God." (James 4:2b) How many times do we complain about what has happened or what we don't have, before we've even talked to God about it? Could it be that like my husband that stressful night, He's ready to help the moment we ask, while instead of doing the reasonable thing and asking, we resent and complain, because our attention has once more been sidetracked?

Prayer and the ADD Mind

As I learned that Thanksgiving Eve, we can miss a lot simply by not asking. One would think that after having a multitude of prayers answered, I would know to ask. And being a greedy, never-satisfied lover of answered prayer, you'd think I would never run out of things to pray about.

Never underestimate the distractibility of the ADD mind.

Last year I was writing a message about prayer. There was a deadline, and as I considered new approaches I wondered, *What would happen if I didn't bother with an outline or revising but just wrote down my thoughts as they came?* The resulting message revealed a great deal about my thought processes. It went something like this:

> "Aren't you glad God loves everybody, even people with ADD? I was actually relieved when found out there was such a thing as adult ADD. I remember thinking, "Well, that sure explains a lot . . ." before my mind was off and running to another subject.
>
> ADD stands for Attention Deficit . . . Have you seen the movie "Up"? Remember the dog in that movie that obviously had ADD? He'd be running along with the others, right on board, and suddenly,—"SQUIRREL!" and he'd be gone. Wasn't he cute? So was that little fish in "Finding Nemo," who definitely had a problem with short-term memory. What was her name? I forgot . . . anyway . . .
>
> When you actually do have these personality traits, it's not always cute or funny. When it comes to prayer, it can be a real guilt trip. I hear about these people who can pray for six hours straight. These super-saints get up around 4 AM, and

they not only pray, they *fast* and pray . . . I'm pretty sure that mean no coffee. How do they *do* that? I'm lucky if I can go from one end of the house to the other and have a clue what I came for.

When I talk to someone I don't know very well, I can usually stick to a logical sequence of questions and information, but with certain friends, one thing will remind me of something else, which will remind me of something else, and by the time it's my turn to say something I seem to be totally changing the subject. I have one or two really good friends who won't even flinch when I do that. We'll just keep on the same train of thought going full speed down the track while our husbands look at each other with glazed eyes, obviously still at the station. They say men's and women's minds work completely differently, but I digress. (So what else is new?)

Back to prayer . . . I know it's crucial. What's a relationship without communication? And what relationship is more important than a relationship with God?

For some reason, when I'm talking to God, my mind is even more random. Even my best girlfriend probably couldn't follow my train of thought sometimes when I'm praying for someone and suddenly I'm asking God questions like "How come the prodigal son's older brother wasn't invited to the party? They just left him out in the field working! And then we criticize him for having a bad attitude?! I'd have an attitude problem, too, if my only brother had been missing for years and finally came back and nobody even told me there was a party going on!"

Have you ever tried to really be organized in your prayer time? Have you ever had everything written down in a nice neat list that you can check off one at a time after you've prayed for each item? I have those lists, and I really should date them, because they are all over the house, and when I come across one marked "URGENT!" it'd be nice to know if that's a request from yesterday's Bible study or last year's Christmas get-together. Putting things on computer is supposed to cut down on paper, but I'm always thinking "What if the computer crashes?" so I make hard copies of everything and then forget where I've filed them, or that they even exist.

Oh yeah, prayer . . . I sometimes wonder if my apparent ADD (I have to say "apparent," otherwise I'm making a negative confession, and that drives certain Christians crazy and makes them think I'm guilty of negative thinking, and I've got enough to feel guilty about, thank you.) . . . I sometimes wonder if my *apparent* ADD is a tool of the devil to keep me from praying, so any time I hear about a new gimmick—a new method of prayer that comes on the scene, I grab hold of it and try it to see if it'll help me get my devotional act together.

"Come before His presence with singing!" (Psalm 100:2a, RSV) OK, I should sing first. So I get out my guitar and start praising God, but once I get started, I could sing to Him for hours, so there were days I never got around to the prayer and Bible reading, and you've got to have prayer and Bible reading, or you've got two more reasons to feel guilty . . .

"You need to thank God before you ask Him for anything new. Otherwise you're being ungrateful!" OK, I don't want to be ungrateful, but I'm one of the most blessed people in the world, so that could take days, too. Besides, once I start thanking Him for my children and grandchildren, I always think of a reason I should call one of them . . . next thing you know I'm on the phone, and I'm *not* talking to God."(From "Prayer, the Temple, and ADD," 2012)

Well, you get the idea. If you relate to that struggle, know that you are not alone! So, what do we do with all the distractions that actually pull us away from prayer?

1. Do realize that God loves you, with all your quirks, struggles, and failings. In other words, **ditch the guilt!** Confess the sin of prayerlessness, if necessary, and then thank Him that "If we confess our sins, He is faithful and just and will forgive us our sins and purify us from all unrighteousness." (I John 1:9) Remind yourself as often as necessary that you are saved by what *He* has done to purchase your forgiveness, not by anything you have or haven't done. Accept that forgiveness and *move on.* Today is a new day.

2. Ask God for discernment in dealing with the distractions. It may be that the thoughts that are distracting you are actually promptings of the Holy Spirit to pray about those things. Know that sometimes it's OK to ditch the list. Ask for wisdom to know if a thought is the next topic of prayer to be prayed over immediately, or a needless distraction, to be dismissed as soon as possible. Thank Him that "If any of you lacks wisdom he should ask God, who gives generously to all without finding fault, and it will be given to him." (James 1:5) In other words, He *wants* you to have wisdom, so this is something you can pray for with confidence!

3. Take concrete steps to eliminate as many distractions as possible. Turn off the phone and let voicemail get it. Keep paper and pen handy for any thoughts that come to you regarding mundane things that need to be added to your to-do list, so you can jot them down and set them aside.

Turn off the TV, computer, and radio. As silly as this sounds, when I get my list of prayer requests that come weekly via email, I actually print them off onto scratch paper so I can close my computer ASAP. I know that the longer I stay on line, the greater my chances of getting sidetracked onto Facebook, Yahoo News, other emails, etc.

If you think of something you just *have* to text someone, compose the text and save it in drafts to send later, so you aren't starting a dialogue while you're trying to pray.

Some of us enjoy good preaching and Bible teaching on TV or radio, and these can become an instance of the good robbing us of the best. There's plenty of technology available today to record these things to listen to later while sorting laundry, but don't interrupt your time *with* God to listen to someone else talk *about* Him.

4. If praying silently you find your mind wandering, try praying out loud. For some of us, it helps to hear ourselves talking to God.

5. For some people it helps to get together with a prayer partner, and pray out loud together. If you are on the same page, you may find yourselves finishing each other's sentences, with one person putting into words what the other is struggling with. What your prayer partner is praying could remind you of something else—pray about that. I have a prayer partner that I can pray with for an hour or more this way,

6. If your mind tends to wander more during physical inactivity, try taking a prayer walk. After all, we walk and talk with our friends, why not with God? If during a "prayer walk" you find you're distracted by something you see, instead of letting it throw you off, make that a matter of prayer, too. It may be that God is leading you to pray for the people who live in the house you're passing or for the former employees of the establishment that just went out of business. And prayer doesn't have to be all asking.—It shouldn't be. While walking you can thank God for that beautiful sunrise, the funny antics of the squirrels, or the sweet fragrance of the lilacs you just passed. I can't imagine being annoyed with someone for stopping in mid-sentence to thank me or praise me for something. By the same token I have a feeling praise and thanks are always appropriate when talking to God.

Remember, prayer is a conversation with your dearest Friend, and most conversations have little surprises (or big ones) along the way. By freeing yourself of preconceived notions of what your prayer "ought to" sound like, or perceived obligation to take a certain stance and speak a certain style, you may find that prayer comes a lot more naturally than you ever thought possible when you just speak from your heart. And if you aren't able to rid yourself of all distractions, you may find that with God's help you can turn them into part of a productive prayer time.

Chapter Three

BARRIER
#3

WRONG MOTIVES

"When you ask, you do not receive, because you ask with wrong motives, that you may spend what you get on your pleasures."

James 4:3

". . . whatever you do, do it all for the glory of God."

I Corinthians 10:31

"Why do you ask?"

When we lived in St. Louis, I used to listen regularly to a pastor on the radio who received prayer requests and prayed for people right there on her program. She wasn't a name-it-and-claim-it preacher, although many times people did call in with some exciting testimonies of how they had received a break-though after being prayed for. One thing that interested me about this program was the way the reverend would bluntly speak the truth—often a truth that the person on the receiving end was not expecting and not exactly comfortable with.

I recall one day when a listener called in who had been healed previously, but after some time of relief, the affliction had returned, and she wanted to be prayed for again. The caller was asked to look up a verse of scripture, and for some awkward moments I could hear her scrounging around, vainly searching for her Bible, while the television was clearly audible in the background. As expected, when the caller returned to the phone, the reverend had a few words for her regarding her priorities.

"Honey, God didn't heal you just so you could watch television more comfortably."

Jesus healed many people during His ministry on earth, more than we can cover here, but a look at a few of the stories can give us good examples of *why* Jesus healed them. It wasn't just so they could heave a sigh of relief and go home to live a selfish life.

One day Jesus saw a funeral for a man who was the only son of his widowed mother. The way society was in those days, a woman with no man to protect and provide for her was bound to be destitute. "When the Lord saw her, his heart went out to *her*" (Luke 7:13a, italics mine) The man was raised from the dead and given back to his mother, presumably so he could care for her.

When Jesus healed Peter's mother-in-law, "The fever left her and she began to wait on them." (Mark 1:31b)

When Jesus healed Bartimaeus, immediately "he received his sight and followed Jesus along the road." (Mark 10:52b) Time and again, people were delivered from their troubles so they could follow Jesus, serve Him, and testify to the world about Him. Some, like the man born blind, found a new kind of trouble and made some enemies among the religious establishment. (John 9) But the privilege of being touched by Jesus outweighed any other desire in his life; "the man said 'Lord, I believe,' and he worshiped him." (vs. 38) Whatever you are asking for in prayer, it should be something that will enable you to be a better follower, better servant, better worshiper of Jesus.

Knights in Dingy Armor

In the popular movie "A Knight's Tale," the knight, William, has one desire—the love of the lady Jocelyn. Or at least he *believes* that she is his one desire. He has trained long and hard for the impending tournament and is confident he can defeat all the others and win her hand. But the lady seems unimpressed with his declaration of love, even annoyed with his boasting. Finally in desperation he cries "What can I do to prove my love for you?" It is then that she drops the proverbial bomb.

"If you love me, fight poorly. Lose."

William cannot believe she is serious, but she insists. In order to prove to her that he loves her, he is to go out and lose. He wrestles with the proposition, then in frustration he declares defiantly, "I *will not* lose!"

Lady Jocelyn looks him in the eye and declares with equal defiance, "Then you do not love me."

At first it seems the lady is a few bricks short of a castle, but as I thought about it, I concluded, *She's a genius!*

Think about it. A knight could fight to win a tournament for many reasons—riches, ambition, pride, success, gloating privileges, all the glory that goes with being the victor. Winning the lady's hand could be just an extra bonus. But Jocelyn doesn't want to be a perk. She wants a man who will love her more than *anything*—more than wealth, popularity, admiration—more than himself and his own ego. Her request is brilliant! It also says something about *her* priorities when it comes to love. Most ladies of the day would be proud to be won by the best, most popular, most glorious knight, but she would rather have true love than the prestige of being the champion's lady.

[Spoiler alert] The day of the tournament, William rides out with much fanfare, amid the shouts of his many admirers, while Jocelyn sits in the gallery looking bored. But when it comes his turn to fight, much to the dismay of his squires, William allows himself to be struck without any resistance whatsoever. After numerous harsh blows, his bewildered squires cry, "Why are you doing this?!"

"I don't know!" he cries, as bewildered as they are.

But Jocelyn knows why, and suddenly she is interested in the tournament. Unable to sit, she jumps to her feet. But then, apparently weak in the knees, she leans against a post for support. As she watches her knight passively receiving the beating of his life, she murmurs incredulously, *"He loves me!"*

OK, so what does this have to do with prayer?

EVERYTHING.

So much of what we pray for seems at first glance so righteous, but more often than we'd like to admit, beneath our pious requests are motives that are less than what our Lord would desire. Christians, especially

American Christians, seriously underestimate the differences between the ways of the world and the ways of the kingdom of God.

From the day Jesus entered the world in the flesh, the way He did things was the direct opposite of what people expected of the Messiah. The King of the universe was born in a barn. He was raised in a humble home, hung out with the lowliest people. And how did He prove His love for us? Not by wiping out His enemies in a glorious show of power, but by allowing Himself to be beaten, mocked, spat on, stripped naked, and nailed to a cross to die a criminal's death.

As I watched William taking a beating for the lady he loved, I had a sense of déjà vu from another film, "The Passion of the Christ." I remembered as I had watched the portrayal of Jesus taking so much abuse without resistance, I was acutely aware that He could have stopped it any time He chose to. He could so easily have been the conquering hero, the glorious Victor. But He wasn't—*not yet.* And like Jocelyn, I was awestruck as I realized—*He loves me!*

Even more awesome is His command that we are to love one another *as He has loved us.* Jesus was God in the flesh, yet "he did not consider equality to God a thing to be grasped, but made himself nothing, taking the very form of a servant." (Philippians 2:6 & 7) Before the Last Supper He washed His disciples' feet (John 13: 4 & 5), doing the job of the lowliest slave. His disciples certainly weren't expecting Him to do it, but Jesus made very clear the role that humility was to play in the life of anyone wanting to be His follower.

> When he had finished washing their feet, he put on his clothes and returned to his place. "Do you understand what I have done for you?" he asked them. "You call me 'Teacher' and 'Lord,' and rightly so, for that is what I am. Now that I, your Lord and Teacher, have washed your feet, you also should wash one another's feet. I have set you an example that you should do as I have done for you. I tell you the truth, no servant is greater than his master, nor is a messenger greater than the one who sent him. Now that you know these things, you will be blessed if you do them."
>
> John 13:12–17

Husbands, you are commanded to love your wives *as Christ loved the Church.* (Ephesians 5:25) Would you be willing to humble yourself to do something for your wife's benefit, even if it meant having your friends poke fun at you and call you "hen-pecked?" Ladies, would you be willing to serve your husbands, even if it meant your more feminist friends might accuse you of being a "doormat?"

Jesus puzzled many people with His teachings, such as "The last shall be first." Could it be that the greatest blessing we can ask of God isn't helping us produce the #1 gospel song, write the latest Christian bestseller, or become a preacher in a mega-church (for *His* glory, of course)? Are we willing to lay aside our desires for such things if He asked us to? Could we be just as happy serving Him, even if it meant cleaning toilets, changing diapers, or caring for a dying patient?

There's nothing wrong with praying for the big stuff—*if* we're asking for the right reason, and *if* we are *called* to do that. But are we open to the possibility that the Lord may have a different calling on our lives, one with a lot less visibility and immediate reward?

The eleventh chapter of Hebrews, known as the "Faith Hall of Fame," lists people like Daniel and Elijah who performed great feats for God—or *He* performed great feats *through* them. We may expect God to be pleased by those who succeed, who win the awards and the fame, more than the more low-profile ones. After all, their high-profile success gives them a "platform" by which they can share the gospel. But that kind of purely numbers-based strategy is the world's mindset.

This chapter in Hebrews ends with a list of nameless "losers," the ones who were persecuted, destitute, hated for the gospel. The Church in the Third World is full of these kinds of saints. And Hebrews says of them, "the world was not worthy of them." These "losers," may be nobodies in the eyes of the world, but though they aren't named in the Bible, you can be sure God knows their names and values them more than we can imagine. They're the kind of people of whom God could say, "They love Me!"

Are *we*? Are we the kind of followers who make it all about Jesus? Or are our prayers all about us, just wrapped in a spiritual package? Remember, anything or anyone more important to you than God—including yourself—is an **idol**.

It's Not About Me

An amazing maturing took place in my daughter Kelly over the summer of 2013. It seemed to revolve around her new mantra, "It's not about me," a concept that was behind every instance where I noticed a difference in the way she was responding to things. And thankfully, it started rubbing off on me.

CTS, the sort of "Christian boot camp" Kelly was involved in all summer, focused a lot on service—service that was both Christ-centered and other-centered. One morning Kelly was on her way to run, thinking the team was leaving in an hour to paint a house, but then she saw them leaving. When she said something about joining them after her run, the leader commented that Kelly was willing to serve—*when it was convenient for her. Ouch!* (Apparently they also emphasized blunt honesty.)

She skipped the run.

That summer the migraines hadn't taken a vacation. I got a text from Kelly one morning saying she had a bad headache, and later I learned they were doing some painting with fumes that aggravated it. I asked if there were some other service she could perform—gardening, raking, washing dishes, something away from the fumes. Her response: "It's not about me."

I thought, *OK, who are you, and what have you done with my daughter?*

Kelly left CTS briefly at the end of July to go to St. Louis for a family wedding celebration. We shared a hotel room with my sister Susie from Arizona, who rolled in after Kelly and I were asleep .

Susie is my only sibling, and we don't see each other nearly enough. When we do, we talk fast and non-stop, with much enthusiasm. There was only one problem with this: Kelly does *not* like talk first thing in the morning. Especially when she wakes up with a migraine, she could be extremely irritated by *any* talk, much less the kind of excited chatter my sister and I were engaging in that first morning. I was sensing that my daughter didn't feel good, and was curbing my yakking, but Susie was oblivious and kept talking excitedly. I knew what was coming next—or I thought I knew.

Now the old Kelly would have exploded. ("Do you *mind?!* Mom, you *know* talking gives me a headache in the morning! Why are you doing this to me?! Would you *please* just *shut up?!* Don't you care about me at all?!")

But this was not the old Kelly. Instead, what we heard was:

"Hey! . . . I *love* that you two love each other and enjoy talking to each other so much! I'm glad you're having a good visit. But I'm not feeling too good, so I'm just going to head down to breakfast now. Take your time and have a good visit."

And she left the room with a smile. ("*Who was that*?")

Now Kelly isn't the only one in the family who benefited from CTS training. She brought home the principles she learned, not only "It's not about me," but the brutal honesty, too. I've had her nail me a few times, and once I got over the initial sting of being corrected by my 21-year-old daughter, I've had an opportunity to grow as well.

I had been involved in the youth group at church for several years—ever since the old Kelly granted me permission to participate—as long as I was not the leader of *her* small group. As an author and speaker, I wanted very much to use my gifts to speak to the youth, and for the past two years the youth pastors had finally granted me the opportunity to do so—once a year. I tried to be grateful for the annual chance to speak my heart, but I couldn't help noticing another leader who spoke to the kids at least once a *month*. Of course, he was a high school teacher . . . but so was I. And he taught speech and drama . . . So did I. So how come he was given so many nights?

That year I emailed the youth staff and asked if there was any chance I could speak more than once a year, and they responded, yes, maybe I could speak *twice* this year—once in the fall, and once in the spring. They had already planned their topics for the semester, and they sent me a schedule for the fall. The majority of slots had already been filled, four of them filled by—you guessed it.

I was confessing (or complaining) about this to Kelly as we walked down the beach, and I wondered out loud if this man was really that much better than I was. Other than a beard, what did he have that I didn't?

I should have seen it coming.

"Mom, it's not about you." (*She's right!* I thought.) "There was a need, and it's being filled, so that's good, whether it's you speaking or someone else."

True! So I'll just pray that he gives a good message, and the kids benefit from it.

Although I hadn't quite arrived, I knew that once this attitude was well established in me, it would be liberating. Already I was feeling freer than when I was grousing about not getting to do more.

The lesson wasn't quite over, however. Soon after that I had a vivid dream, where our neighboring town of St. Clair was stirring with excitement about a production that was to be performed on Halloween Night, entitled "Satan's Worst Nightmare." Something was very familiar about this, and that was the fact that this was *MY* production that ***I*** had directed for fifteen years!

If I may back up a moment and give some real-life background: For fifteen years I had worked with a large team of enthusiastic performers and other workers, complete with a live band, free refreshments, and free Bibles and tracts. "Satan's Worst Nightmare" had become a tradition in St. Clair, and I hadn't even minded its being called "the Tuckers' outreach," since I'd been partnering with Kelly and Ray Tucker, who always held the event in their front yard. Every year we had seen around 700 people passing through, seeing the Resurrection reenacted, hearing the praise and worship music, and receiving literature that we hoped would lead them into a saving relationship with our Lord. In fact, it seemed every year we received word later about people who had made decisions to follow Christ from seeing our production.

And now (in my dream) there were posters all over town that we had never authorized, people we didn't know announcing an organizational meeting, and everyone was acting as though this were some novel happening in their town!

I decided to attend the meeting just to see what was going on, and sure enough, it was MY "Satan's Worst Nightmare"—same songs, same choreography, under the direction of *that man!* And everyone was excited and praising that man for having such a great idea. I told Kelly Tucker about it, and was surprised to learn that she had not been invited to the meeting, either; neither had any of the dedicated families who had faithfully served with us in the outreach year after year.

That man hijacked our outreach! I was more than a little indignant, and I was sure I had grounds for complaint, maybe even legal action.

"I'm almost certain we have that material copyrighted," I told Kelly, and I began rifling through my files until I found the "script." The title at the top of one page read in bold print: "SATAN'S WORST NIGHTMARE."

"Here it is!" I declared. I scanned the page, looking for the copyright notice. Finally I found a small note at the bottom of the page that said "NOTICE: . . ." *OK, here it is . . .*

". . . This production is to be used to spread the gospel of Jesus Christ."

Reality hit as if my daughter had just said to me—again—"Mom, it's not about you."

No, it isn't, is it? I thought. And at that moment I gave "my baby" to God—as if it hadn't been His property all along. And at the very end of the dream, when I saw "*that man*" posting another massive poster regarding the biggest production St. Clair had ever seen, I was able to say, "These posters look great. I really hope this outreach is a huge success."

Now I'm *really* hoping that I can keep up that "It's-not-about-me" attitude in my waking life as well!

Reality Check

If you have been praying for a long time for something that you are convinced is God's will, with no visible results, it may be time to examine your motives.

Even in praying for others there can be selfish motives. Does your vision of someone's coming to Christ include that person's admitting you were right? In your dream for her, does her testimony include mentioning you by name? Would you relish the admiration of friends who praise your faithfulness in praying for that person?

In other words, are you really seeking the Lord's will and His glory, or would you be happy to share some of that glory (humbly, of course)?

Would you be just as joyful if after years of prayers and witnessing *someone else* had the privilege of leading that person to Christ? How would you feel if that "baby Christian" you've been praying for suddenly had a thriving ministry spring up overnight that dwarfed the ministry you've been laboring over for half your life? How would you feel if that person wrote a book that was much more successful than yours, a book in which you were not even mentioned in the credits? Would you rejoice if the struggling person at work that you've prayed for got promoted ahead of you? . . . You get the point.

It might be a good thing to pray regularly before asking for anything—for yourself or anyone else—"Lord, I give you my heart. Purify my desires, my affections, my motives, and my attitude." Otherwise, when your prayers are fulfilled you may find that you're less than delighted with the answer.

Chapter Four

BARRIER #4

WRONG THING, WRONG TIME

". . . if we ask anything according to his will, he hears us. And if we know that he hears us—whatever we ask—we know that we have what we asked of him."

I John 5:14b, 15

We saw in John 17 that in His final hours Jesus expressed His desire to be one with us. Now, if we are one with God, as He wants us to be, when we pray, we'll be asking Him to do the very things He desires to do, and has wanted to do all along.

I know what you're thinking—*He's God, so why doesn't He just do it?*?

I have a simple answer to that:

I have no idea.

For some reason He wants us to ask, so we can have a part in what He's doing—which is actually pretty amazing. Think about it—we get to be partners with God! As the kids would say, 'How cool is that?!"

Have you ever had something happen that was obviously an answer to prayer? It's a great feeling, isn't it, knowing that you've played a part in God's plan?

On the other hand, how many times have you prayed and *not* seen an answer? I'm guessing pretty many. It's probably the reason you picked up this book, and it's my reason for writing it. Unanswered prayer is a problem for most if not all Christians today.

I really think we Americans have a distorted view of prayer and its purpose. Maybe it's because we're used to getting what we want yesterday. We have everything from digital cameras, to ATMs, to websites for downloading music so we don't have to drive somewhere to buy it, etc.

Maybe it's because we're seeing prayer as a way to "get stuff from God," which is seeing ourselves *apart from* Him, instead of being *one with* Him. I hope by the end of this chapter you'll be seeing it differently.

In this chapter I want to focus on the idea of **praying God's will**, because God has promised that if we pray *according to His will,* He will answer.

(I know, it sounds like a Catch 22—"I'll do what you want as long as you ask me to do what I wanted to do anyway." But bear with me . . .)

We've got to start with the premise that *God is God.* As obvious as that sounds, it means that we have to have faith that He knows a lot more than we do. And if we believe that, it's not a huge step to believe that His plan is infinitely better than anything we could think up. If we ask Him for something and don't see it, it doesn't mean He hasn't heard, doesn't care, or is unable to fulfill our request. It means that either

1. we've asked for the wrong thing—and trust me, if we got it, we wouldn't be happy in the long run, or
2. we've asked for it at the wrong time, or
3. —and here's the really exciting one—He has an idea that's even *better* than what we had in mind!

Sometimes His perfect will isn't what we have in mind because to get to God's best often involves a lot of pain, waiting, or both, and frankly most of us would rather be comfortable, skip the hard part, and settle for mediocre. (Face it, we're cowards.) But if we're willing to trust Him enough to hang in there, I think we'll find it well worth it. Ephesians 3:20 refers to "him who is able to do immeasurably more than all we ask or imagine."

I think one of the best examples of this truth is found in the book of Genesis, in my very favorite story in all of the Old Testament—the story of Joseph.

When the time isn't right

For those who may be unfamiliar with this story or who have forgotten the details, Joseph was the favorite of Jacob's twelve sons. He was the first-born of Rachel, Jacob's favorite wife. (He had been tricked into marrying Rachel's sister, but I'll let you read about that on your own.)

Jacob was not very subtle about his favoritism; you probably have heard about the "coat of many colors" he gave Joseph, which made it disgustingly obvious to everyone that Joseph was Daddy's favorite. Predictably, his brothers resented him for it.

Joseph was not very subtle, either. He had dreams indicating that his brothers, and even his parents, would bow down to him, and he foolishly blabbed about it to everyone. Later all of Joseph's brothers, with the exception of his little brother Benjamin, sold Joseph into slavery, tore his coat, and covered it with goat's blood. They then took it home and told their father that a wild animal had eaten Joseph.

Joseph was taken to the house of one of Pharaoh's officials named Potiphar, but the Bible says that God was with him, and because God gave him favor with Potiphar, Joseph was soon put in charge of the whole household.

Well, it so happened that Potiphar's wife was impressed with the young Hebrew slave, too. She found Joseph extremely attractive and tried often to seduce him. Joseph never gave in to her, saying that it would be violating Potiphar's trust *and* sinning against God for him to do such a thing. But she was not one to give up.

One day the would-be adulteress found Joseph alone in the house and grabbed him by his cloak. Even then Joseph did not give in but fled the scene, leaving his cloak in her hand. When Potiphar returned, out of spite she accused *Joseph* of assaulting *her*, and Joseph was thrown into the dungeon!

Before you conclude that character doesn't pay, you need to hear the rest of the story.

Even in the prison God was with Joseph, and he won the favor of the jailer, who gave him authority over the whole prison. (Sound familiar?)

Now two servants of Pharaoh himself, the baker and cupbearer, were also imprisoned, and one night they each had a dream that they couldn't interpret. This really upset them, because in those days dreams were considered messages from the gods. When they told Joseph about the dreams, God gave Joseph interpretations to both of them. Joseph correctly predicted that in three days the cupbearer would be pardoned and returned to his former position, but that the baker would be executed. Joseph pleaded with the cupbearer to tell Pharaoh about his situation when he was freed in the hope of getting him released.

Three days later the baker was executed, and the cupbearer was restored to his former place. But incredibly, the cupbearer forgot all about Joseph (Genesis 40:23)!

Poor Joseph spent another *two years* in that miserable prison before he saw any answer to his prayers. (Can you say *you* would have held onto your faith that long?)

One night Pharaoh had two dreams that troubled him deeply.—Remember, in that culture, dreams were very significant. How much more significant were the dreams of Pharaoh? In the turmoil of the following morning, the cupbearer finally remembered Joseph! At last Joseph was brought out of the prison to try to give an interpretation. It is a scene of profound irony—Pharaoh, king of the most powerful nation in the world, looking to this slave-prisoner for direction.

The first dream showed seven fat cows coming up out of the Nile, followed by seven emaciated cows that ate up the fat ones, yet stayed as scrawny as they has been from the start. The second dream was similar: seven full stalks of grain, swallowed up by seven shriveled stalks that stayed shriveled.

After humbly acknowledging that interpretations are from God, Joseph stated that Pharaoh's dreams were indeed significant. He told Pharaoh that both his dreams predicted the same thing—that there would be seven years of plenty for Egypt, followed by seven years of famine. He advised Pharaoh to put a "discerning and wise man" in charge of storing up grain during the years of plenty and distributing it during the years of famine.

Pharaoh took Joseph's advice and immediately put someone in charge, and it doesn't take a rocket scientist to guess who was chosen. Joseph received probably the greatest single promotion in history—He went from an imprisoned slave to second in command of a huge, prosperous nation. Later, through his position he was able to save the lives of his whole family—not to mention all of Egypt and the rest of the world—and to reconcile with the brothers who had sold him into slavery. If you haven't read the story, or if it's been a while, check it out. There's plenty more drama after that.

For instance, when Joseph's brothers came to Egypt to buy grain, they didn't recognize him. Joseph, now fluent in Egyptian, spoke to his brothers through an interpreter that he didn't really need. The brothers had no idea that when they spoke among themselves, the "Egyptian lord" could understand every word they were saying!

Joseph wasn't playing some cruel game with his brothers. He wanted to know if they had changed any since selling him into slavery, and he spent a period of months putting them through some very elaborate tests, and freaking them out on more than one occasion—such as seating them in their exact birth order at the table, and giving their innocent brother Benjamin five times as much food as the rest of them!

For Joseph, keeping his identity from his brothers was stressful; a couple of times he had to excuse himself to go somewhere private and weep. Finally, when he was convinced that his brothers were not the same men who had sold him into slavery, he revealed himself to them. Anyone who knows this story is familiar with Joseph's words at the end of Genesis: "You intended to harm me, but God intended it for good . . ." (50:20)

I have read the story of Joseph countless times, but it never ceases to thrill me, possibly because I myself was a rather naïve, spoiled child that has had some growing up to do. Possibly it's because I myself dream a lot and have known what it's like for God to speak to me through dreams, both mine and others'—always confirming His written Word in Scripture, of course!

But I think the biggest reason I love this story, and why so many people love it, is that this young man had to go through so much suffering, and yet because he hung onto his faith during the darkest times, his story has a happy ending. Even though I know the ending—and every detail leading up to it—I never get tired of reading it (I usually read it very slowly, because I can't just read a story, I have to direct the movie in my head!).

Recently I was indulging in the sheer drama of it, as I read how Joseph, betrayed, enslaved, and falsely accused, was now thrown into prison. I pictured him getting his hopes up when he was able to interpret the dreams of the baker and the cupbearer. As usual, I was extremely *frustrated* by that *bone-headed* cupbearer's *forgetting* to mention Joseph to Pharaoh! As usual, I marveled at Joseph's faith through two more years in a miserable prison—and wondered if I could have held onto my faith for that long.

But that day, as I read about Pharaoh's dreams and the cupbearer's *finally* remembering Joseph, I realized something that had never occurred to me before, at least not in connection with this story—

God's timing! It got me thinking about some *what-ifs* . . .

Joseph no doubt wanted the cupbearer to mention him right away, but what if this had happened? I stopped reading to imagine the scenario:

PHARAOH: "I'll have that wine now, cupbearer."

CUPBEARER: "It's good to be back, Your Majesty. Um . . . an interesting thing happened in prison. The baker and I both had dreams a few nights ago, and there was this prisoner named Joseph who interpreted them for us. He predicted that the baker would be executed but that I'd come back to serve you. Pretty remarkable, wouldn't you say . . . Sir? . . .Your Majesty?"

PHARAOH [*absently*]: "That's nice. . . . Uh, are you gonna give me that wine now?"

CUPBEARER: "—Oh! Sorry, Sir . . . Here . . ."

I'm not sure what Joseph was hoping for from that encounter, but I have a feeling it wouldn't have happened.

Or what if it *had* happened the way Joseph had hoped? What if the cupbearer had acted a little more shrewdly and had picked a better moment to bring up Joseph's situation—*assuming* he had that kind of influence on Pharaoh, *and assuming* he cared enough about Joseph to stick his neck out for him?

> **PHARAOH** [*with slightly slurred speech*]: "This is exceptional wine! I'll have a third cup."
>
> **CUPBEARER** [*to himself*]: "Fourth, but who's counting? [to Pharaoh] Yes, Your Majesty."
>
> **PHARAOH:** "This wine has me in a good mood. I feel like doing something [*speaking the word with some difficulty*] magnanimous today. Any ideas, Cupbearer?"
>
> **CUPBEARER:** "Well, Sir, it's funny you should ask. There's this man in the dungeon named Joseph. He seems like a decent guy. He was Potiphar's slave. He was charged with assaulting Potiphar's wife, but knowing him, I can't believe he would have done such a thing."
>
> **PHARAOH:** "Hmm . . . Sounds like Potiphar wasn't too convinced, either, just throwing him in jail. He's had slaves executed on the spot for less than that."
>
> **CUPBEARER:** "This Joseph is an amazing interpreter of dreams, too. The baker and I—"
>
> **PHARAOH** [*impatiently*]: "What are you jabbering about now? Never mind all that. Just give me another cup of that wine, and then tell the jailer I want to see him. If it means that much to you, I'll let this slave go back to Potiphar's house."

Back to Potiphar's house . . . Of course, if Joseph got out of prison, that's probably where he would go. Where else would they send him?

Let's stop and think for a moment what *that* little reunion might have looked like:

POTIPHAR [*wryly*]: "Well, look who's back."

JOSEPH: "Yes, Master. I want you to know that I—"

POTIPHAR: "Joseph, this is Onan, my *new* head servant. [*ONAN, a huge, intimidating slave steps forward.*] Go with him to the slaves' quarters.

JOSEPH: "Yes, Master." [pauses] "Sir, I don't have a cloak."

POTIPHAR: "Cloak? [chuckling] Oh, you won't need a cloak. You'll be hauling water this morning."

JOSEPH [*deflated*]: "Oh . . . yes, Master."

POTIPHAR: "And this afternoon you'll be cleaning out the horses' stalls."

JOSEPH [*miserably*]: "Yes, Master." [*He and Onan start to leave.*]

POTIPHAR: "Oh, and Onan . . . [*glaring at Joseph*] Keep this one away from my wife."

ONAN: "Yes, Master."

POTIPHAR: "He's not to go near the house. He can sleep in the barn."

Is it just me, or does that not look like much of an improvement? At least in the prison he had some respect.

(Here's a thought—have you ever considered that it just might turn out to be that much of a disappointment if God gave *you* what *you're* asking for? . . . Just something to think about . . .) But getting out of prison was actually Joseph's "Plan C."

"Plan B" was not to be falsely accused and imprisoned in the first place, to stay the head servant in Potiphar's house. He would have been better off, but he still would have been a slave.

Joseph's "Plan A," of course, was not to have been sold into slavery to begin with, but to stay at home and continue being Daddy's favorite—not knowing, of course, that a famine was coming to wipe them out. In fact, any of Joseph's plans would have had the same eventual result: starvation for everyone, including himself.

But what if *God* had *another* plan, way better than any of Joseph's plans—more than Joseph could ever have imagined? What if while Joseph was spending another two years in the dungeon, forgotten by everyone except God, God's plan involved something infinitely better?

Like having him become Prime Minister of Egypt and save the world?

But here's the point: **God's plan requires God's timing**.

Notice that God *waited* until the moment Pharaoh was *desperate* for an interpretation of his own dreams. *Now* He had Pharaoh's attention!

It could well be that the cupbearer wasn't a bonehead after all; maybe God *caused* him to forget about Joseph until the time was just right. And when that moment came, the fog was lifted, the cupbearer remembered, and Joseph was brought out of the dungeon. (Genesis 41:14).

But let's consider just one more scenario—one more "what if." What if during those two years Joseph had abandoned his faith? After all, who could blame him? His God had allowed all these horrible things to happen to him. Even when he had gotten his hopes up with the cupbearer, it was only to realize over time that he had been forgotten. God didn't seem to be answering his prayers or caring about him at all, did He? What if those two years had made Joseph bitter toward God, and by the time he was brought out he wasn't thinking about God at all?

PHARAOH: ". . . So, that's what I dreamt last night. I hear you can interpret dreams. Is that true?"

JOSEPH: "Well, Your Majesty, I don't like to brag, but I do have quite an ability to predict the future based on people's dreams."

PHARAOH [*impatiently*]: "Then *do it!* What do my dreams mean???"

JOSEPH: "Well . . . um . . . They mean . . . er . . . uh . . . >*sigh*< . . . I have no idea."

PHARAOH: "*GUARDS!* Take him back to the dungeon, he's wasting my time!"

[*Seven years later JOSEPH starves to death with the rest of the world.*]

But as we know, that's *not* what happened. When Joseph was brought out of the dungeon, his faith was miraculously still intact, and when asked to interpret Pharaoh's dreams, he humbly replied, "I cannot do it . . . but God will give Pharaoh the answer he desires" (Genesis 41:16). And in one morning he went from being a prisoner to second in command of the greatest nation of his time!

(Does that make you wonder what *you* might have missed those times you gave up on God?)

A Double-edged Sword

God's timing—our faith. His perfect plan requires both.

How many times do we ask God for something and get frustrated because we don't get what we ask for right away? How many times, even as we remember how "in all things God works for the good of those who love him," (Romans 8:28) we might roll our eyes and mutter something sarcastic about His teaching us patience? (Well, I've done that, anyway.) Could it be that the problem isn't that we're asking too much from God, but too *little*? Could it be that if we are willing to wait for *His* timing, we might not only gain strength and maturity but also see answers to our prayers that are "immeasurably more than all we ask or imagine"? (Ephesians 3:20)

The Gift of a Nation

Saeed Abedini is an Iranian American pastor who was arrested and imprisoned in Iran for his Christian faith. He has suffered beatings, isolation, even torture, and has been told by his captors that he could be released and go home, if he would just renounce his faith in Christ. He has refused.

Saeed's wife Naghmeh has prayed earnestly for his release, as have thousands of Christians, and his continued incarceration has been heartbreaking for his family. But Naghmeh has shown astonishing courage and perseverance through it all, even appearing before the United Nations to plead for her husband's release.

On September 17, 2013, the one-year anniversary of her husband's arrest, Naghmeh shared with an audience at Liberty University about how God is doing "exceedingly abundantly beyond" what she has been asking for, in answer to a childlike prayer she prayed years ago as a little girl:

> He's allowed me to preach in front of over 100 nations. I was present in June, and I was speaking in front of the United Nations in Geneva, and over 190 countries are there, and I got to tell them that Jesus Christ is the way to God, and He's the God of peace they're looking for. And you know Saeed and I always dreamed to reach millions of Muslims for Christ. I got to do that. I got to go on media like BBC Farsi and Voice of America Persia that broadcast to Iran. Over fifty million Iranians got to hear me on live TV as they were watching, to tell them about Jesus Christ, so I praise God for that . . .
>
> I don't have a ministry. I'm just a girl who loves Jesus . . . Psalm 2 says, "Today I have begotten you. Ask of me and I will give you the nations for your inheritance." . . . I would ask the Lord when I was 9, I would say, "Lord, give me the nation of Iran for my inheritance. I want it!" I didn't see it until this year that I got to speak to millions of Iranians. I've led so many Muslims to Christ. Saeed and I have led hundreds and hundreds of Muslims to Christ . . ."

As Naghmeh will tell you, even in the midst of tremendous pain, God's plans can take us beyond our wildest dreams. I can't tell you how many times, I've been deeply disappointed, then ended up later (sometime *much* later) saying to my friends—and anyone else who would listen—"You won't *believe* what God just did!!!"

So . . . are we ready to submit our requests to Him, then to submit *ourselves* to Him? To be "one" with Him, even if we don't know exactly what that will mean for us in the future? Are we willing to trust that a delay doesn't mean He hasn't heard us or doesn't care or isn't answering our prayers? (You may be asking the Lord for a person, when He wants to give you a nation!)

And now I'd like to get personal for just a moment . . . There are two things I have been praying about for a long time that are very important to me, very close to my heart. One I've been praying about for more than seventeen years now, and the answer may be getting close. The other I've prayed about for around forty years.

I'm still waiting for that one.

Now before you conclude that I'm an idiot, wasting my life and my prayers, I should also tell you that I could sit here for another 500 pages or more telling you about all the prayers that *have* been answered for me in the meantime.—and those would just be the ones written about in my journals! Yes, I get discouraged, impatient, and frustrated at times. I do get tired of waiting, and I'm quite capable of throwing a pity-party for myself from time to time. But those times are getting less frequent, and for the most part, my relationship with God is sweeter than it has ever been. He has done some incredible things in my life. (I once asked Him to move Lake Huron 200 feet—and He did!—long story, which I'll share in a later chapter.) And yes, He has been teaching me faith and patience and perseverance through those prayers that haven't been answered—*yet*! I figure if He can answer a million little prayers, and a few hundred not-so-little ones, I'm sure He can and will answer those other two—in His own way, in His perfect timing. And deep down in my heart of hearts, that's what I really want—His perfect will, and to be the kind of mature, patient, persevering woman of God He wants me to be, not the pouting little baby that complains because things aren't happening fast enough.

Worth the Wait

Recently on a glorious June morning in St. Louis, seven members of our family were savoring their last precious moments together before scattering to return to our homes in four different states. We were enjoying an elegant Iranian-style brunch at the home of my cousin Tom and his beautiful bride Tayebeh, or "Tay" as we call her. The deck was near enough to completion that we could eat there, surrounded by Tom's sculpture, fragrant jasmine, and other potted plants. The yard was in the process of being landscaped, and the interior of the house had already been remodeled and redecorated. Tom's house had always been what one would call "eclectic," but since Tay's arrival it had been transformed, and definitely leaning in the Middle Eastern direction. Everywhere there were exquisite Persian rugs, tapestries, silver, and other exotic gifts from Iran. Out on the deck the breakfast table was bursting with food, stories, and laughter.

Everyone agrees that Tom and Tay are a perfectly matched couple, and the transformation of Tom's home has gone far beyond mere decoration. Ever since their wedding celebration a year before—a multicultural event with people from all over the world dancing to Iranian, American, and European disco music—Tom has been happier than I've ever known him to be. He had always been well liked, funny, and attractive, and to some it was a puzzlement why he had remained single for so long, especially a creative, fun-loving man who got along so well with children. (Actually, he's kind of a big kid himself.) Since Tom had been well into his sixties and seemingly had no interest in marriage, the family had pretty much written him off as a life-long bachelor, especially since he had been diagnosed with a form of blood cancer, giving him much more pressing things to think about than dating.

But God has a way of blessing us when we least expect it. That morning we were bringing in the tiny Turkish coffee cups, the star-shaped plates with nuts and raisins, the basket of breads, and the platter with the remains of the fresh fruit back into the kitchen. I took in the beauty of the decor, smelled the jasmine, heard the laughter, and felt the love in that home, and I was overwhelmed with the way God has blessed my cousin.

"Tom, just think of the difference between your life now and ten years ago—or even *five* years ago!" I marveled.

Tom knew exactly what I was referring to—his precious wife. His face lit up with joy as he suddenly exclaimed, as though he were realizing it for the first time, "And all because I got sick!"—*That's true!* I thought.

I remembered that when Tom was first diagnosed, we had all prayed for his healing—*the sooner the better*, we thought. The instantaneous healing hadn't come, though, and along with his various treatments Tom had gone to the hospital for one particular medical procedure. When the anesthesia wore off, he had found himself looking into the eyes of a beautiful Iranian nurse, and it had been love at first sight. ("And the rest is history.")

Today he has a wonderful wife, grown children, and a little granddaughter to play with—"instant family!" He now has extended family all over the world as well.

I'm sure Tom would tell you God's best is worth waiting for, even waiting until the "tender" age of 66 to marry the love of his life.

God's Two-part Plan

God is perfectly capable of multitasking. *While* He is growing us by making us wait—teaching us patience and making our faith stronger—it could well be that at the same time He is also preparing something for us far beyond our wildest dreams! If we just hold on, the way Joseph did, we just might be overwhelmed by what turns out to have been God's plan all along.

I think it's worth a try, don't you?

Chapter Five

BARRIER

#5

WRONG PRIORITIES

"Set your minds on things above, not on earthly things."

Colossians 3:2

"But seek first his kingdom and his righteousness, and all these things will be given to you as well."

Matthew 6:33

"But our citizenship is in heaven . . ."

Philippians 3:20a

What Else Matters?

It was the morning of the National Day of Prayer. I was sitting in the auditorium at City Hall, listening to my daughter's school choir singing a goose-bump-raising rendition of "You Are God Alone." They were warming up for the city-wide prayer meeting that was starting in half an hour. And I was crying.

My daughter Kelly had been having a rough time in high school. The migraines that had first appeared when she was 4 years old had continued to plague her through grade school and middle school and had caused her record absences through high school, in spite of years of prayers and attempts to find a solution through medicine, both traditional and "alternative."

But in spite of enduring more pain than some people suffer in a lifetime, Kelly had found a few sources of pleasure in her life. By far her greatest joy was singing, and her favorite part of school was choir. When the students performed, Kelly's face radiated with unmistakable joy. She had looked forward to the National Day of Prayer and taking part, and as I had said goodbye to her that morning and she left for school, I had whispered a prayer of thanks to God for this special day.

My optimism was short-lived, however. Kelly had called me from the parking lot of a McDonald's half a mile from school to tell me about the migraine that had assaulted her shortly after she'd walked out the door. When I had suggested that she come home, take some medication, and rest until the assembly, she had sobbed that if she didn't show up at 8:00 she wouldn't be allowed to sing with the choir.

There are definite advantages to a small Christian school, one of them being teachers who know each student well and practice grace along with discipline. As I called the office to explain Kelly's dilemma, the choir director, who "happened" to be right by the phone, responded with compassion. She said to let Kelly come home, take a pill and a nap, and meet the choir at City Hall at 11:30 if she was feeling better.

But the medication that knocked out the migraine had a way of knocking out the patient as well, and when I had tried to rouse Kelly for the prayer meeting, she had been hopelessly (and predictably) dead to the world. Now as the choir finished their warm-up and filed off the stage, there I sat, with nothing to do but feel sorry for Kelly, thinking of all the important high school events she had missed and would never again get a chance to do. And yes, I'll admit I was feeling pretty sorry for myself, as well. (When "BabyBear" hurts, "MamaBear" hurts, too.) So in spite of my efforts to contain them, the tears flowed.

I was digging through my purse, looking for a tissue when I came across my small New Testament. Since the prayer meeting didn't start until noon, I knew I had twenty minutes to kill, and the last thing I wanted to do was to spend them wallowing in self-pity. So I pulled out the Bible and prayed.

Lord Jesus, please encourage me. I don't want to feel this way today!

I was not in the habit of looking for answers to problems by haphazardly opening the Bible; I hadn't done that since college. But since I wasn't sure what I was looking for, I opened the Book at random, planning just to read until I found something helpful, or until the prayer meeting started, whichever came first.

The scripture that first caught my eye was the last chapter of Mark.

> When the Sabbath was over, Mary Magdalene, Mary the mother of James, and Salome bought spices so that they might go to anoint Jesus' body. Very early on the first day of the week, just after sunrise, they were on their way to the tomb and they asked each other, "Who will roll the stone away from the entrance of the tomb?"
>
> But when they looked up, they saw that the stone, which was very large, had been rolled away. As they entered the tomb, they saw a young man dressed in a white robe sitting on the right side, and they were alarmed.
>
> "Don't be alarmed," he said. "You are looking for Jesus, the Nazarene, who was crucified. He has risen!"
>
> Mark 16: 1–6

Something told me I had seen enough, so I stopped reading.

OK, what does that have to do with Kelly's migraines? I wondered. But then I pondered the significance of the passage.

Jesus is alive. . . . *JESUS IS ALIVE!* That means death is not the end . . . for Him *or* for us! And it certainly means this life isn't the be-all and end-all for those who trust in the Lord.—It's barely the beginning!

Yes, my daughter had missed the National Day of Prayer, over a hundred days of high school, and numerous weekend festivities. She had missed Homecoming, but someday she would be at the greatest Homecoming in history. She had missed singing in the choir that day, but someday she would sing in heaven's choir forever. Kelly loved Jesus, and she would get to spend forever with Him, at the never-ending, greatest celebration of all time. When one had that to look forward to . . . What else mattered?

What else matters? I asked myself, and I found that in spite of my pity-party, I was smiling. I decided that I would pour myself into the Day of Prayer and keep a better perspective on life from that day on, by remembering the one thing that really matters—*Jesus is alive!*

What *doesn't* matter has a way of getting to us, though, and it was only a couple of days later that I was charging out of the house to escape the stress for a while. I figured pedaling my bike at top speed to the health club and working out with weights was better than screaming at people, but at the moment my pedaling was accompanied by angry muttering under my breath.

Along the way, I noticed the grass in front of the high school was littered with small pieces of paper, but I was too preoccupied with my own frustration to think much about it. But after a workout had melted away some of the aggravation, I realized as I passed the school again on my way home that the Gideons must have been there handing out Bibles, and obviously someone had not appreciated the gesture. Dozens of pages torn out of a small New Testament had been strewn all over the lawn. I slowed my bike down and looked sadly at the precious scriptures fluttering in the wind. I could almost see the devil smiling.

Well, somebody is going to get something from this Bible! I thought with righteous defiance. I stopped, picked up a couple of pages, and a sense of deja vu accompanied what I read on one:

> On the first day of the week, very early in the morning, the women took the spices they had prepared and went to the tomb. They found the stone rolled away . . .
>
> Luke 24:1–2

My mouth dropped open, and tears filled my eyes as the words reverberated in my mind: *What else matters???*

Okay, Lord. So my short-term memory needs some work . . .

Not only do we err in God's timing, but I believe we frequently misunderstand His priorities as well, probably because as we saw in Chapter Two, we are seeing things from an earthly perspective. Yes, God delights in healing people of their diseases. Yes, He delights in prospering us materially. But "It is not God's will that any should perish," that is, perish *eternally*. When everything is going smoothly, it's easy to forget about God, or at least put Him on the back burner.

In the Old Testament God was constantly warning the children of the Israel of the *dangers of prosperity*. Moses pleaded with the people not to forget the Lord when they had times of plenty and ease in the Promised Land, and again and again they did just that. The pattern repeats itself throughout history: God blesses His people; they become comfortable; they stray from Him; He disciplines them; they repent and come back to Him; He blesses them again; again they get comfortable and stray. In reading the history of the Israelites, I have been astonished that they never seemed to catch on. It could be because, while I was reading a condensed history of the people, they were living out their lives, day-to-day, without stepping back to look at the Big Picture—the *eternal* picture.

Then I realize it isn't just ancient Israel's nature; I have seen the same pattern in recent history in the US. God has blessed this country more than any other, and over time our culture as a whole has drifted away from Him, with occasional milestones, such as legalized abortion and the banning of prayer in public places, that indicates which direction we are going.

Occasionally there is a disaster that makes headlines—a shooting at Columbine High School, a bombing in Oklahoma City, mass murder on 9-11—and for a while the churches in America overflow with people grieving, searching, maybe even repenting. But it isn't long before most of them get back to "business as usual," with attention to God relegated to one hour on Sunday morning, if they think of Him at all.

I have often wondered what it would happen if people came to love the Lord in the hard times, but then *continued* to love Him, even in the good times.

We may never know.

On a smaller scale, take the example of a woman who is praying for her son to know the Lord. Maybe he has known and served Him before, but in times of prosperity he's now distracted by work, vacations, entertainment, money matters, and everything else that comes with an affluent lifestyle. The devoted mother faithfully continues praying that God will get his attention.

Then one day the diagnosis comes: terminal cancer.

And *now God has his attention!*

And what is the request that the prayer team gets? "Pray for healing!"

Now please don't misunderstand—I'm not at all against healing—I've been healed on several occasions, and I'm thankful to God for it. It has enabled me to serve Him with more physical energy and strength. And I do pray that my friends and acquaintances who struggle with sickness will be healed. But I have another prayer for them that I consider far more significant.

Think about it. Which is worse—having cancer, dying at age 50 knowing God, and spending eternity in heaven,—or living in good health for 100 years without any regard for God, then spending eternity in darkness and regret? I realize it doesn't have to be one or the other, but it does seem a little ironic that we pray fervently for God to get someone's attention, and once He does it, we immediately cry out to Him is, in essence, *"Make it stop!"*

After many years of unsuccessful prayer for sick friends, I have changed my approach. Acknowledging that God is ultimately in control, that He has a plan, and that He probably knows way more about what that person really needs than I do, I pray:

"Lord, whatever You want to accomplish with this sickness (or job loss, or other trouble) I pray that it will be accomplished in Your perfect will, in Your perfect timing." And the sooner that is accomplished, the sooner the trouble can be done with and victory celebrated.

I have even come to the point where I can pray for myself with this eternal perspective, although sometimes I let immediate pain keep me in the *make-it-stop!* mindset, which usually just prolongs the agony and afflicts those around me with my bad attitude at the same time.

Well, one cure for a bad attitude is the realization that I can't make it by myself. Pride and independence has no place in the life of a child of God.

In America we celebrate our independence, and in a certain context, we should. But both as a nation and as individuals, we are helplessly *de*pendent upon God; we don't take our next breath without His giving it to us. None of us is self-sufficient, and yet most of the time we are allowed to walk around believing that we are. Sickness, loss of a job, or other calamity is a potent reminder that we rely on the Lord for *everything,*—and we always have. As we turn to Him and acknowledge that we are completely dependent on Him, we discover that He is completely depend*able.* And, as we stop struggling and remind ourselves that He loved us enough to die for us, we can be assured that He will move in our behalf and do what's best for us, whether or not we understand what is going on at the moment. With that letting go, there is peace.

If your prayer list is filled merely with things that would make your life and the lives of those around you easier, it could be that you need a fresh perspective—an *eternal* perspective—and think about what *God* wants—what *He* would consider most important. You may find that you need to step out of your comfort zone to reach out to people who need to know Jesus. While it is good to pray for their healing, a gesture of kindness from you, done in Jesus' name, could cause that person to look to Him and make an impact that will last far beyond a physical recovery. That time of hardship could turn out to be a turning point in that person's life—in his eternal destiny. And where people spend eternity is God's #1 priority. After all, He was willing to die to make the difference.

I recently heard a Bible teacher point out that we rarely, if ever, hear a testimony from someone who came to know the Lord in good times. Usually the testimony starts with something like, "I thought I had it all together and didn't need God, so I didn't give Him a thought. Then my world fell apart . . ." And the person goes on to describe how he came into a saving relationship with the Lord.

By all means, pray for people who are sick to be healed, for those who have lost jobs to find work, and for families in hard times to see their situations get better. But *first* pray for those people to know God, and if they already do, pray that their relationship with Him will grow stronger and sweeter through the difficulties. These times, whether hard or easy, will someday be gone in the blink of an eye. Their only real value is how they impact people *for eternity.*

"But I thought . . . !"

The contrast between our priorities and God's can also be seen when our plans and expectations encounter a glitch. It is then that we have a choice whether to let it frustrate us, or to allow it to teach us something about the mind and priorities of the God we want to serve.

I was bringing up my children "in the nurture and admonition of the Lord," but I wasn't dictating their choices when it came to things such as when and where they would be baptized. I did pray that they would take that step, and I looked forward to seeing them baptized and giving their testimonies.

So when I learned after the fact that my sixteen-year-old son had been baptized, I was disappointed and a little hurt that I had not been there, until God made me realize that the important thing was that *he was baptized.* The Still, Small Voice pointed out something else to me as well: The fact that he was baptized *without me* was testimony to the fact that it had been *his* decision, not mine. So, in spite of my thwarted expectation of how it was "supposed to be," my prayers were answered in a very real way. My son had made the decision I was praying for. And I am ever grateful.

Nancy's Story

A more dramatic example of God's priorities' trumping ours is a sudden and unexpected situation encountered by my friend Nancy, an American missionary in Guatemala.

The year her son Hank graduated from high school Nancy was headed for the airport to return to the States for what was expected to be a joyous event, but within moments her plans were to be derailed.

Making her way along a winding mountain road, Nancy saw another car careening toward her, obviously out of control. She pulled to the shoulder to avoid being hit but was struck by the other vehicle anyway. When the dust settled, her car was dangling precariously at the edge of a ravine.

Nancy managed to get out of the car without its plunging down the mountainside, but her problems were only beginning. The three men in the other car, predictably drunk, got out and offered Nancy a check to cover the damage in an attempt to avoid police involvement. Knowing that the check was likely worth less than the paper it was written on, and unaware of the procedure in Guatemala regarding auto accidents, Nancy chose to involve the police. A short time later she was having second thoughts about that decision as she was being fingerprinted at the police station. She quickly learned that in Guatemala auto accidents were dealt with by jailing all drivers until things could be sorted out. In other words, every driver was guilty until proven innocent.

Those of us back home who got the news began to pray immediately against what we saw as an interruption in Nancy's life, an *obstacle* sent by *the enemy* to rob her of the joy of being with her son on his big day! I'm pretty sure none of us considered the possibility that what was happening could be used by God, maybe even had been His plan to begin with. I suspect it was even harder for Nancy to discern God's working in the nightmare that followed her "arrest." Likely our prayers were all similar—that the issue would be settled quickly, so Nancy's life could get back on track, with her at her son's graduation, *the way it was supposed to be!*

But God apparently had a different approach: "'For my thoughts are not your thoughts, neither are your ways my ways,' declares the LORD." (Isaiah 55:8)

To understand this dichotomy, it might help to have two perspectives. Let's start with Nancy's.

What began as a promising day—a mother's anticipating with pride seeing her son graduate—turned into a day of suffering one indignity after another. Being fingerprinted by foreign police was only the beginning. When Nancy told them she needed to use a restroom, she was told at first that there wasn't one. When she asked the obvious question, they admitted that they had one, but said that it didn't work very well and that they would not let her use it. When her situation got desperate, she was marched outside with two guards, who never took their eyes off her, and made to relieve herself in the street at gunpoint!

One of the men had been taken to the hospital, and nothing could be sorted out until he was released. One of the other men tried to get Nancy to state that the accident had been her fault. When she refused, she was treated to a string of obscenities. Since the jail was a men's jail, it was decided that Nancy wouldn't be jailed there, and she was allowed to spend the night in her disabled Jeep, which was around the corner where it had been towed. She was escorted there—again at gunpoint, and it was there that she got a little sleep, with orders to be back at the police station at 5 A.M.

Early the next day the man who had been sent to the hospital was released, and the three men then decided among themselves which one of them would claim to have been the "driver" (not the one who had actually been driving), while the other two were free to go and seek legal counsel. In Guatemala, one was also responsible to find his/her own lawyer. Nancy, being alone, was stuck at the police station. Apparently this was going to be more than a brief interruption in her trip.

Nancy expected that she would be allowed one phone call. (At least criminals are allowed a phone call in all the movies.) Since the police station had no phones, she was escorted through town (at gunpoint, of course) to the public phone company. A North American man who worked for the local cable company ran up and asked what was going on. Providentially, he knew the judge and said he would speak to him about her situation. Nancy was able to reach Van, a missionary friend, who immediately set out to come to her aid. Meanwhile, a local lawyer who had heard what was going on came by and informed the police that as a North American Nancy had a right to use their bathroom, but she still was not given anything to eat. Eventually she was released in the custody of Van, and was somewhat relieved to be able to spend the night at his house (complete with food and a bathroom!) instead of in jail.

The next day Nancy was given paperwork to sign with vague statements about the accident that omitted some of the "details," such as the fact that the other driver had been inebriated at the time of the crash. As infuriating as it was to sign the papers, Nancy just wanted to get the whole nasty business behind her and get home to the States, ASAP.

There were more complications at the airport that I won't go into—Nancy has written her own book, entitled *But God,* which tells the story in more detail—but suffice it to say that getting home was no easy feat, and left her with both jail time and fugitive status on her record!

(I gained a bit of knowledge from this story that I probably will never need: Not everyone with a criminal record in Guatemala has necessarily done anything wrong to deserve it!)

OK, we probably can understand the extreme aggravation of this turn of events. But is there an "up side?"

First, I think Nancy would want me to point out that the situation was not all bad, and in retrospect she is grateful for several things. The first and most obvious, of course, is that her car did *not* fall off the mountain. This was especially important, not just to Nancy, but to the people who lived in the houses below! Secondly, as degrading as it was to have to use the street for a restroom, Nancy was grateful that she always wore a skirt. (Do we need to explain?) The fact that Van was a faithful friend and available when she needed him was a huge blessing, not to mention the North American man and the local lawyer (angels?) that just "happened to be" in the right place at the right time and stepped in to help her.

Still, we might ask, how could this travesty of justice possibly be God's plan for one of His children—for a *missionary*, no less? To discern the "God scenario" in this story, it might help to see the event from another perspective, from that of a certain Guatemalan man whose name I don't know. I'll call him "Marcos."

Marcos was a Christian, although one could scarcely tell by his behavior. Despite his earlier good intentions, Marcos made the mistake of hanging with the wrong friends. I'll call them "Juan" and "Pedro." Juan and Pedro were men who liked to engage in risky behavior, such as drinking and reckless driving. Before long Marcos was—literally *and* figuratively—heading full-speed in the wrong direction. In American "Christianese," Marcos would be called "backslidden."

The carelessness of Marcos and his friends had caused fender-benders in the past, but they had never felt the full brunt of the consequences, since Marcos didn't mind a few dents in his car, and Juan or Pedro always "made it right" with their checkbooks. No one who knew Guatemala's approach to auto accidents ever wanted to involve the police, and the trio would soon be on their way.

This particular day, however, they had no such luck. After colliding with an American woman on a winding mountain road, they found her unwilling to take the check. Marcos was taken to the hospital with minor injuries, and Juan and Pedro were taken to the police station with the American woman.

The next day, as the effects of the last night's binge wore off and physical pain set in, a few facts hit Marcos like thunder. Even with his foggy memory, he recalled the spot on the familiar road where the collision had taken place, and where the woman's car had been when the dust cleared. Marcos began to shake as he realized that had she not been there, he and his buddies would have plunged to their deaths, and would be facing their Maker in a deplorable spiritual state. As if for extra emphasis, lest he miss the point, he was reminded that the woman he had hit was not only a Christian but a *Christian missionary*! Or perhaps she was even an angel!

After his release from the hospital, under heavy conviction from the Holy Spirit, a broken and repentant Marcos bought a cup of coffee and took it to the woman in her Jeep, where she had spent the night, with a contrite apology and a solemn promise that he would return to church.

That day was the last Nancy saw of this man, and whether or not he kept his promise and got back on track, we don't know. He certainly didn't stand up to his buddies when they planned their less-than-honest strategy the next day. But it doesn't take a huge leap of faith to believe that the whole situation was part of God's plan to get the attention of this stray lamb in hopes of bringing him back to the fold—not to mention saving the lives of all three men! After all, human souls are God's first priority, mattering to Him even more than a parents' getting to a son's graduation. (Of course, it's easy for me to say. It wasn't *my* son's graduation.)

The story of "Marcos" is reason enough to believe that the accident in the remote mountains of Guatemala was actually not an accident at all. But there is even more to this story.

Nancy's friend Van is an evangelist, one who never misses an opportunity to share the gospel with anyone and everyone. During Nancy's ordeal, when Van had some time with the two other men from the accident, he actually was able to witness to all the men in the jail—and, to make a long story short, he led *thirteen* of them to Christ! (Can you hear the angels rejoicing?!)

In our subjective little worlds, we can get hung up on things like getting to an event, accomplishing a certain task, being with certain people at a certain time, or otherwise following our own agendas. And when our plans get derailed, our first response is to protest, or in the case of the "spiritual" people, to pray that things will get back to what they were "supposed to be!"

But stories like Nancy's have convinced me that I in fact *have no idea* what's "supposed to be" most of the time! It is then that praying simply, "Thy will be done" becomes something that is more than simply "blind faith." It is a faith that acknowledges that God can and will use us for greater purposes than we have in mind, *if* we just trust Him—and not fuss when we don't get our way! There is so much more to God's will than our comfort and convenience. Far better than comfort and convenience is the ability to see the Lord at work and be in awe of His ways, even and especially in life's little unpleasant surprises.

(By the way, Nancy did get back in time for Hank's graduation, but I am confident that even if he had graduated without his mother present, she would be no less proud of him.)

God's Priorities

Once I began to know the Lord, I began to realize that He really does care about me and that He actually does hear and answer prayer. I got excited, to say the least. And it's not in my nature to keep that kind of stuff to myself. "Witnessing" came easily for a storyteller like me. There were those who would write off my experiences as "coincidence," but I could see that the more I prayed, the more "coincidences" I saw. And if I stopped praying, I stopped seeing "coincidences." But when I started praying again, there were "coincidences" again! (How's *that* for a coincidence?) So the doubters and cynics didn't get me down. I knew what had happened to me—*I was there!*

But there's something in human nature (well, in *me*, anyway) that can easily start putting too much emphasis on the miracles, even the coincidences. Yes, Jesus did miracles, giving evidence to those around Him that He was God in the flesh. Naturally, people flocked to Him, especially hungry people who had heard He fed 5,000 and sick people who had heard that He healed. Even when He was on trial, Herod was hoping to see Him perform a miracle, like a court magician.

But whenever Jesus' teachings began to get hard, the crowd thinned out fast.

Even His disciples started to have their priorities slip during the height of the ministry. As His followers, they had been given authority over all the power of the enemy (Satan). So they went out to heal the sick. They did as they were told and came back beside themselves with excitement, having discovered that the power given to them was far beyond their expectations—they were even able to command demons! Who *wouldn't* let that go to their heads?

> The seventy-two returned with joy and said, "Lord, even the demons submit to us in your name."
>
> He replied, "I saw Satan fall like lightning from heaven. I have given you authority to trample on snakes and scorpions and to overcome all the power of the enemy; nothing will harm you. However, do not rejoice that the spirits submit to you, but rejoice that your names are written in heaven."
>
> Luke 10:17–20

Notice that Jesus acknowledged the truth of their observations, but He was quick to remind them that as wonderful as miracles are, the biggest privilege of all is to be saved. After all, the Sermon on the Mount makes it clear that just because someone can perform miracles doesn't mean that person is saved.

> "Not everyone who says to me, 'Lord, Lord,' will enter the kingdom of heaven, but only he who does the will of my Father who is in heaven. Many will say to me on that day, "Lord, Lord, did we not prophesy in your name, and in your name drive out demons and perform many miracles?' Then I will tell them plainly, 'I never knew you. Away from me, you evildoers!'"
>
> Matthew 7:21–23

Some of the most godly Christians I know are those who have held onto their faith through good times and bad and have loved and served

God without *ever* performing any kind of "miracle."

Someone may be able to put on a spectacular show, even do it in the name of Jesus, but such a display is short-lived. Heaven is forever.

A Rude Awakening

A pastor once told me about an incident at a church whose congregation tended to be self-righteous and smug. Fed up with their self-satisfied attitude, the minister stepped to the pulpit one morning and shocked them out of their complacency.

"Every day," he said, "thousands of people in this world die and go into a Christ-less eternity. And most Christians don't give a s__."

As he had expected, there was a loud collective gasp from the congregation, so much that a stray cat passing by outside got sucked right into the church. (OK, I made that part up, but you get the point.)

After the shocked silence that followed, the preacher leaned over the pulpit, made sure every eye was on him, and continued.

"And do you know what *really* bothers me? You're more upset that I said that word than you are that thousands of people are dying and going to hell!"

He nailed them.

I never found out whether that message resulted in repentance and more concern for humanity, but I would hope that at least some of those people were willing to rearrange their priorities and make them more like God's.

God's Priorities

Some other examples of God's priorities:

Justice, mercy, and faithfulness matter more than tithing down to the last speck of spice in the garden and other nitpicky practices. (Matthew 23: 23, 24)

What's inside matters more than what's outside. (Matthew 23: 25, 26)

People are more important than animals. One man meant more to the Lord than a herd of pigs, although the townspeople's values seemed the opposite. (Matthew 8: 28–34)

Maybe "blood is thicker than water," but spiritual relationships matter more to Jesus than biological ones. (Luke 11: 27, 28.) Please know that this doesn't mean Mary wasn't blessed. She was! But it wasn't because she was Jesus' biological mother. It was because she heard the word of God and obeyed. (Luke 1: 38)

What a person *does* with what he has matters more than how *much* he has. (Mark 12:41–44; Matthew 25: 14–30)

Someone's soul matters more than his stuff. (Matthew 16: 26)

What's in a man's heart matters more than what's in his stomach. (Mark 7: 15)

The eternal soul matters more than the physical body. (Luke 12: 4, 5)

Being in the world and being protected from the evil one can be better than being taken out of the world. (John 17: 15)

And as we've seen, Jesus' emphasis on the unity of believers without a word about their being "right" all the time (John 17) shows the importance of grace and love over religiosity; harmonious relationships in the Church take priority over worship. (Matthew 18:15–17)

The disciples expressed God's priorities as they went out into the world when the Church was in its infancy:

Obeying God matters more than obeying man. (Acts 5: 29)

Paul cared little how he was judged by a human court. God's opinion mattered more than anyone else's. (I Corinthians 4: 3, 4)

Paul knew he should be provided for, but he was willing to go without rather than to hinder the gospel. His mission mattered more than his pay. (I Corinthians 9: 12)

Paul valued speaking in tongues and prophesying as gifts from God, but he clearly stated that prophesying in an intelligible language was far better than wowing people with tongues. (I Corinthians 14: 5, 19)

Most important of all is what we see in the Garden of Gethsemane, that Jesus did *not* want to go to the cross if there had been another way to save us. (Matthew 26: 39) Since Jesus' prayers were always answered, we call conclude that *there was no other way.* So He went to His death. Apparently saving us was more important to Jesus than getting out of being crucified! Think of what that says about how much He loves us!

So, pray as much as you want, but let's keep first things first.

Chapter Six

BARRIER

#6

LACK OF FAITH

[Jesus] replied, ". . . I tell you the truth, if you have faith as small as a mustard seed, you can say to this mountain, 'Move from here to there' and it will move. Nothing will be impossible for you."

Matthew 17:20

Stop Wishing

"Ann, I wish I had your faith!"

This was not the first time this person near and dear to me had expressed her desire to share the blessings I was enjoying, and it wasn't the first time I had tried to explain to her that *she could!* I tried to think of another way—some way I hadn't used yet—to explain to her that faith is a *choice*, a choice one makes independently of feelings, but once again my words seemed to fall on deaf ears.

"I just can't get myself to feel the way you do," she confessed, and I tried not to scream in frustration as I explained, *one more time,* that faith is not a feeling, it's a *choice*. Unfortunately it was a choice I couldn't make for her, a choice she once again did not make that day.

I'm afraid the problem of the lack of faith in America stems from the widespread misconception of what faith is. Faith is too often portrayed as a strong, often irrational feeling that builds until it finally explodes into some sort of miracle, sort of an emotional version of the Big Bang. But that isn't what faith is at all. Faith happens when we act according to what we *know* about God, and it stands to reason that the better we know God, the more faith we are able to have. The people I know with the greatest faith also have the greatest love for the Word of God, the Bible. After all, how are we supposed to have faith in a promise without knowing what it is?

If you aren't sure what God wants for your life, it's time to dive into His Word. Don't be worried that you're not a Bible scholar. The most important principles in the Bible (like "Love your neighbor") are easy to understand. Our problem isn't what we don't understand in the Bible, our problem is not obeying what we do understand!

Once you know some things about what God desires in you, it's time to put them into practice. This is stepping out in faith! It doesn't matter if you don't *feel* like it; in fact the less you feel like it, the more faith you're showing in your obedience. God honors your *willingness* to obey, not the fact that obeying happens to fit your mood that day. Don't be surprised if what starts out feeling counterintuitive leads to some spiritual discoveries along the way. The greatest spiritual discovery for me was that *God can be trusted; my emotions can't.*

Which is Better?

It was the last day of class, closing out my first year as a "real" (certified) teacher. It was a bittersweet day, as this was the first group of students I had ever taught that I considered *my kids*. I had taught other classes in the past—music, French, English, and speech—but this was the first class that had been my very own home room. I had formed a special bond with the twenty-four freshmen, during a year that started out with the shock of 9-11 and ended with my singing them my rendition of "I Hope You Dance," as some girls got teary-eyed and a couple of boys waved imaginary lighters.

The next year they would all be leaving this charter school for other public and private schools scattered throughout the county. Since it was the last day I would ever see them all together, I was anxious to impart to them some last words of wisdom that would go with them and, I hoped, would nudge them toward Jesus. These kids knew what I believed, although I had been careful not to "impose" my beliefs on a captive audience; after all, this was technically a public school. My method of choice was often to ask them questions that would make them think for themselves, and, I prayed, come to the right conclusions on their own.

"Which is better," I challenged them on this last day, "—a *lot* of faith in two *inches* of ice, or a *little* faith in two *feet* of ice?" In Michigan with our lakes and long winters it was a familiar scenario.

Immediately a student or two who knew I was a "person of faith" blurted out, "A *lot* of faith in two *inches* of ice!"

I guess they thought I had some miracle of nature in mind, but I was talking common sense here.

"You're going to get very wet and very cold," I teased. "Think about this: What's going to hold up your weight on a frozen pond, two *inches* of ice or two *feet*?"

"Duh!" laughed one of the other students, proud that he had not blurted earlier.

"Exactly," I explained. "If the ice is two *feet* thick, you don't need a lot of faith. All you need is enough faith to take the first step on it." (I didn't use the term "mustard seed," but they got the point.)

"Remember the terrorists last fall? They had enough faith to hijack four planes and commit suicide! They had a *lot* of faith that they were going to get rewarded for killing all those people. But they were *wrong*." (I was pretty confident I'd get no argument there.)

"Please remember," I concluded, making sure every student was making eye contact with me, "what matters isn't *how much* faith you have, it's putting your faith in the *right thing* . . . or Person," I added, while a couple of Christian students smiled back knowingly.

Too many of us, especially in America, think that faith is some feeling we have to muster up, and when the emotion is intense enough, that's when our prayers get answered because of our "great faith."

Nonsense! As James 2:17 says, ". . . faith by itself, if it is not accompanied by action, is dead." Faith is what motivates us to *action*, no matter how we may be feeling. The friends of the paralytic had great faith that Jesus could heal their friend, but they didn't show it by sitting around letting warm fuzzy feelings build to a crescendo. They cut a hole in the roof and lowered the sick man down to where Jesus was. Now I am not recommending you engage in this kind of vandalism any time soon! I *am* saying that their faith led to *action.*

Did any of them feel any misgivings? Did any of them think to himself, *If this doesn't work, we're in big trouble!*—? We don't know. We haven't been told, because what they were feeling is irrelevant. Any doubts that may have come to them didn't matter, either, as long as their faith overcame them. What does matter is that they took the action that expressed their faith—they brought their friend to Jesus.

I can hear some people saying, "That was then, this is now. Who ever sees a miracle these days?"

I'm glad you asked . . .

The Prayer that Moved a Lake

Perhaps my biggest adventure in faith happened shortly after we moved to Port Huron. We had bought a house on Lake Huron with a beautiful view and a bit of beach out front. I say "a bit," because the lake levels had been consistently rising until on rough days the waves lapped at the small retaining wall at the edge of our lawn. I'm sure all the neighbors were wondering what would happen if and when the water rose to the point of flooding our yards, and in October of 1986, one resident in particular was concerned to the point of suggesting I pray about it.

This suggestion may have been offered facetiously, as this was not a person who prayed, as far as I knew, and one with whom I shared few of my "answered prayer" testimonies.

It was an occasion, however, when a recent answer to prayer had been so remarkable that I couldn't contain my excitement and shared the story with this normally aloof man. Instead of registering amazement at God's goodness, he issued a challenge.

"Well, if prayer is so powerful, are you praying for our beach?"

Good question. I was somewhat taken aback by the words coming from him, but I had seen God work in miraculous ways before . . .

"You want me to?" I asked, watching his expression.

"Sure, why not?" he quipped. "Pray for a hundred feet of beach by next summer." (It was early October at the time.)

"OK," I agreed with a smile. He laughed.

"While you're at it, why don't you pray for *two* hundred feet?" I knew he was teasing me, but I took the bait.

"I will!" I retorted. Then in a burst of either faith or presumptive foolishness, I added, "And you watch! By next summer there *will be* two hundred feet of beach!"

He looked at me with amusement. "Tell you what," he said. "If there's two hundred feet of beach out there by next summer, I'll convert."

Sensing a loophole, I eyed him suspiciously and asked, "Convert to *what*?" He smiled condescendingly.

"Anything you want me to be," he promised.

Whether or not this person was entirely serious, I took his word for it, and wondered what sort of adventure in faith this would turn out to be.

The next morning I was seated in my usual chair for my morning devotions. I turned to the Bible reading for the day, which *just happened to be* (yeah, right.) Matthew 17. Verse 20 fairly jumped off the page, where Jesus told His disciples, ". . . if you have faith as small as a mustard seed, you can say to this mountain, 'Move from here to there,' and it will move. Nothing shall be impossible for you."

I knew my faith was at least as big as a mustard seed; I reasoned, *If I can speak to a mountain, I can speak to a lake.* The only question was, *Is it God's will to move Lake Huron 200 feet?* The idea seemed a little presumptuous, except for one detail: An unbeliever had expressed openness to the God Who could actually answer such a huge request. A verse in II Peter came to mind: "He is patient with you, *not wanting anyone to perish,* [italics mine] but everyone to come to repentance." (II Peter 3:9b)

So there was my confirmation. If this person had been at all serious, this could be the way God finally gets his attention! It certainly was preferable to other ways in which I've known Him to get people's attention. So, down to the water I went.

It was a calm day, and there was a "beach" of about eight feet to stand on. As I stood with my toes at the edge of the water, I prayed that God would move the water back 200 feet. As I expected, I didn't see anything obvious happen, but that little detail didn't deter me. I knew about the importance of persistence in prayer, and I figured I had until June 21 to pray the water back the full distance.

My husband, who has a degree in environmental engineering among other things, subscribed to the Army Corps of Engineers' monthly newsletter, which showed the levels of all five of the Great Lakes. The charts also included projected levels for future months, shown with a dotted line, which that fall was shown ascending ominously toward levels that I considered unacceptable.

OK, so I can believe the experts at the Army Corps of Engineers, or I can trust God's Word.—Hey, no-brainer.

Although miniscule doubts routinely tried to bombard my prayer life, I determined that *when* God answered, the fact that the Army Corps of Engineers had been wrong would make it even more convincing. That skeptical lake-dweller would *have to* believe!

As I may have mentioned, and should be obvious by now, I can be a little OCD, so although I also struggle with ADD, once I get it into my head to start something and stick with it, I can pursue it with great tenacity. Whatever the state of my health, the family's schedule, or the weather, I went down to the water *daily* that winter to pray, command, declare, (whatever it took) to move the water back, one foot at a time.

It wasn't always easy. Sometimes the weather wasn't good, and I would find myself standing in the rain or blown by a cold wind. One winter day there was a near-blizzard blowing, and waves, sand, ice, and snow churned about, seemingly chewing up the shoreline instead of generously depositing sand where it was needed. Bundled up head to toe, I commanded the wind in Jesus' name to "cease and desist!" The following day I learned that the storm had knocked a couple of houses on the Canadian side into the lake, but on our side it looked as if any sand taken from the Canadian shore had been dumped onto our beach and that of our neighbors!

As a mother of small children who was involved in their school and other activities, I had my days pretty much filled up. On more than one occasion I would sink into bed close to midnight, only to realize I had not remembered to pray over the beach that day! Resisting the temptation to just pray in bed, I would throw my winter coat on over my nightgown and trudge out to the lake for my "normal" ritual.

My faith had to withstand a long winter, in which snowdrifts and icebergs built up on the shoreline, so no one could see where the "shore" actually was. On stormy days waves would wash sand up onto the snow and ice, and it was impossible to see how much water, in whatever form, was under the sand. So when the warmer breezes began to blow and the frozen masses began to shrink, I was very interested to see where the shoreline was going to settle. Would we have two hundred feet of beach, or . . . considerably less?

By the time the icebergs were gone, the answer was clear: *Yes.*

We definitely had more beach than we'd had before, but not two hundred feet by a long shot. It was more like seventy-five feet.

However . . .

Fifty feet or so from the shore was a sandbar, a long mass of sand, barely submerged, which stretched along the shore in front of our property and that of some of our neighbors. As the dry spring continued, the sandbar gradually emerged and grew in size until it was more like an island, separated from the land by a small body of water that was becoming smaller every day. By mid-June the water was a mere puddle, and by the first day of spring, (*on the dot!*) it had closed up, and we were standing on—you guessed it—*two hundred feet of beach!* As if to drive the point home, the local paper had a picture of swimmers at the beach just south of our house, alongside an article that stated, "The beach has 200 more feet of sand this year because of the city's erosion control work and a 2-1/2-foot drop in water levels." (It was SO hard not to be smug!)

The next time I saw the skeptic whose off-the-cuff remark started this whole adventure in prayer, he was staring pensively at the lake. As I approached, I wondered if and when I should bring up the topic of our conversation some months back, but as it turned out, I didn't have to.

"Well," he said, "it looks as if you got your two hundred feet of beach."

"Yep," I said. "It looks like God kept His part of the deal. Now it's time to keep yours."

"What deal?" he asked with a blank look on his face

Are you kidding me?!

"Where you said you'd convert . . ." and I repeated the entire conversation. (Never get into an argument with someone with OCD.)

"I never said that," he responded in a tone that started out defensive but quickly turned infuriatingly smug. "I think you must have dreamt it," he added condescendingly. (I'm surprised he didn't pat me on the head.)

I walked away before I could blurt out something I would have regretted.

I was complaining later to a friend with whom I had shared the original prayer request, that *after all that,* this person didn't (wouldn't) come to Christ, but she was undaunted.

"Never mind him. Think of what all this did for your faith," she reasoned.

I thought, *Yeah, big deal.* But since then I have come to realize this was a *very* big deal, even though I had been thinking the conversion of a skeptic was the *biggest* deal. Not only had I seen an answer to probably the most ambitious prayer I had ever stepped out of my comfort zone for, but more importantly.—and here's the point—it was the first time I had established the discipline of examining myself daily. Let me explain.

I don't know if you have ever stepped out and asked God to move a mountain—or as in this case, a lake. But if you have ever considered it, you know that one doesn't approach such a request casually. While this was way before I started researching prayer, I had been a Christian long enough to realize that one doesn't ask God to move mountains—or lakes!—while hanging onto grudges (Mark 11:22–25) or secret sins (Psalm 66:18) or doubts (James 1:6 & 7) or wrong motives (James 4:3). It was also essential to acknowledge Him as the all-powerful One Who could accomplish what is being asked, so besides self-examination, repentance, and forgiveness, each time of prayer was ushered in with some faith-building praise and worship (Psalm 66:17). As I stood at the shore each day, I had purged my soul of anything I was aware of that might be a hindrance, and asked God to cleanse me of anything else of which I might be unaware, until I stood there praising Him with a clean, pure heart.

Please don't misunderstand. It's not that I had discovered any "magic formula" for a miracle, and I hope that no one comes to the conclusion that if we systematically check things off some kind of spiritual checklist that we'll automatically get what we ask for. *God* is still the One in control, and granting a request is still His choice to make. I *am* saying that if we're going to "pray big" we would do well to recognize any obstacles (barriers) in our lives that might get in the way of God's answer. Then whatever the answer is—"yes," "no," or "later"—we can know that it is because that answer is best, not because we messed up somewhere and are coming to God in an unworthy fashion.

Still, the answer may very well be "yes," and you'll laugh at yourself for actually being *surprised* when you get what you asked for!

So this was a huge time of growth in my prayer life—a time I still remember on the occasional summer day when I'm running across our massive beach at top speed, trying not to burn my bare feet on the hot sand that's just a *little too far* from the water!

Miracle or Providence?

Do I believe that having the lake recede 200 feet in one winter was a miracle? Not really, if you define "miracle" as God's intervening by breaking the laws of nature. I'm sure the lake levels went down by purely natural causes. But it doesn't take a violation of God's laws of nature for me to believe He was involved in what happened.

In the Exodus, with the parting of the Red Sea by strong winds that are known to occur in that area, the answer to prayer was not so much the "what," as the "when." God knew what was going to happen with the Red Sea, and the timing of the Exodus was such that the Israelites escaped, while the Egyptians arrived just in time to be drowned as the winds stopped and the waters closed in again.

On a much smaller, more personal level, I believe that God knew what would happen with the Great Lakes and when, and that it would have happened anyway. But in His *providence*, He allowed me to have that conversation with a skeptic that particular fall and to read the scripture the following day about moving mountains that set me off on an adventure in prayer that eventually helped lead me to study what the Bible says about spiritual barriers in order to avoid them. As my friend pointed out, it may not have been so much to put on a spectacle for an unbeliever, but to get me to pay more attention to what He wants from me in prayer—such as faith. Faith in miracles that shatter the laws of nature? Maybe, but not necessarily. Just faith that knows that "... *in all things* God works for the good of those who love him, who are called according to his purpose." (Romans 8:28) (italics mine)

"No-brainer?"

Many times in our lives we are faced with the choice between acting on what we *feel* and acting on what we *know*. My favorite illustration of this principle is one I heard years ago, of the snake in the garden.

Let's say one day I'm in my garden, minding my own business, and my emotions on a 1–10 scale of intensity are at about a "1." I'm content, focused . . .

Then I see it. Not five yards away is a four-foot snake.

I am not a fan of snakes.

Suddenly on that scale of intensity, my emotions shoot from a "1" to a "10." Mentally I'm thinking *danger!* and my mental danger alarm is also at a "10," because I know Michigan has poisonous snakes, but I don't know what they look like.

I am having physical symptoms of panic, as well. My heart is pounding. I'm short of breath. I'd like to run, but all the energy seems to have drained out of my body. So I sit there, frozen, staring at the creature that's staring back at me. It's not moving, but any minute I expect it to lunge in for the kill.

But it never does. And then I notice something that I hadn't noticed before. On the snake's side is what looks like . . . writing. . . . It *is* writing! It says . . . "Made in Taiwan."

OK, so I just had a near heart attack over a plastic toy from the Dollar Store. Immediately my mental danger alarm drops back to a "zero." But oddly, my emotions are not so quick to go back to where they were. I'm still a little short of breath, and my heart is still pounding almost as fast as before. My physical and emotional state is still at a 7 or 8. Calming down is going to take a few minutes.

Meanwhile, I have a choice to make. I could (a) go with my emotions and run screaming into the house, or (b) calmly pick up my shovel and keep planting. Now in this scenario, that's a no-brainer. Who in their right mind would go running and screaming from what they know is a plastic snake? When faced with a choice between acting on what we feel and acting on what we know, we go with what we know.

. . . Or do we?

A favorite ploy of the devil is the thought, *I must not have faith. If I did, I wouldn't feel this way*—as if none of the heroes of the Bible ever felt fear or doubt or confusion. You don't have to read much of scripture to see that these heroic men and women were just as human as we are.

One of the great examples of faith was Job. That poor man went through a living hell, and yet he held onto God. Anyone who has read the book of Job knows that this man experienced intense feelings of anger, fear, and depression, and yet he has been hailed as a hero of the faith, because even in his misery he cried out, "I know that my Redeemer lives" (Job 19:25a)! And when seemingly close to death, he declared, "Though he [God] slay me yet will I hope in him"!(13:15a) The word "will" indicates a choice Job was making that had nothing to do with the despair he was no doubt feeling.

There were days my feelings said to me, *this is crazy!* as I stood on the shore and asked God to move Lake Huron. Apparently it didn't matter; I was still there, doing what I believed God wanted me to do, and my prayers were answered, maybe not miraculously but certainly in an amazing show of His power over nature.

If you are battling the lie that *If I had faith I wouldn't feel this way,* take heart! The mere fact that you are concerned with whether or not you have faith in God or His promises shows that you do! Never mind how you *feel*, what are you going to *do*? Your faith isn't evidenced by the absence of fear (That can actually be evidence of lunacy!) but by the choices you make.

Stop being a slave to your emotions. Step out in faith!

Holding On

"Be patient, then, brothers, until the Lord's coming. See how the farmer waits for the land to yield its valuable crop and how patient he

> is for the autumn and spring rains. You too, be patient and stand firm . . ."
>
> James 5: 7–8a

Sometimes, though, faith doesn't require stepping out. Sometimes it just requires holding on, and even that seems more than we can manage. We forget that faith, by definition, "is being sure of what we hope for and certain of what we do not see." (Hebrews 11:1) If we saw it (Him), it wouldn't be faith..

I think the concept of faith in the midst of trouble was well illustrated by a dream I had not long ago, probably one of the eeriest dreams I have ever had. I had been reading the book of Job, which may have had something to do with the imagery.

The setting was darkness—pitch black darkness. The sky that stretched above me had not a single star shining, and the sea that surrounded me was a black as the sky, with no visible lights or any other sign of land or another boat in any direction. I must have had a small lantern in the boat, because there was just enough light to see my fishing line for a few yards before it disappeared into the inky blackness.

Now here's the eerie part: The line wasn't going into the water but was disappearing into the sky—*straight up*, in fact, and the line was taut; something had a hold of the other end, but it was impossible to see what it was. I was starting to think, *This is getting creepy.*

Then I gradually became aware that there was some dialogue about what was going on. I heard voices, faint at first, then becoming more audible, but I could see no one with me in the boat. It was as though I were on the news, and someone was speculating about the mysterious entity at the end of my fishing line. Listening to the commentary, I quickly picked up that most people, if not the whole population, had come to believe that there was nothing "up there"—no stars, no moon, no sun—so what could my line be attached to?

"It certainly couldn't be God," said one voice authoritatively, "since He doesn't exist," and the other voices murmured their agreement, "No, of course not."

At that point I interrupted the commentary and bluntly asked, "OK, so if there isn't a God, who's got the other end of my line?" I was still holding my end, and although nothing was tugging at it, it wasn't letting go, either. I had a sudden desire to quote Scripture to these people, but of all the verses and passages I've learned by heart, at that moment the only one that came to mind was "Never will I leave you; never will I forsake you." (Hebrews 13: 5b)

At that moment the dream became a little less creepy. As I looked at the line, which appeared to be as fragile as a spider's silken thread, disappearing into the darkness, I knew *He was there,* even if I couldn't see Him, and even if no one else in the world believed He was there. After all, my line was still being held tightly directly overhead, so the burden of proof was on them.

So the dream that started out eerie ended up being strangely reassuring. (If the line had suddenly gone limp and fallen back into my little boat—now *that* would have been disturbing!)

As Job clung to his faith in the midst of the darkest time in his life, he had more than his share of grief, loss, pain, and heartbreak—much of it inflicted by the people around him. But what tormented Job the most was that he couldn't find God. He insisted that God was just, that He knew all things, and that someday he would meet Him face to face, but at the time all he could see was his faith trailing off into darkness. But like a fishing line, Job's faith was much stronger than it appeared, and somewhere on the other end, God was holding onto him, forbidding the enemy to end his life.

The Christian faith is not always a joyride, and the fact that we have been warned that dark times are coming should encourage us that God knows where we are. We need to hold on tight to the lifeline that connects us to the God we can't see, even if there are proud naysayers all around us.

After all, He sees everything, even in the dark.

He loves us.

And He's not letting go.

Chapter Seven

BARRIER

#7

LACK OF COMMITMENT

Then Jesus told his disciples a parable to show them that they should always pray and never give up.

Luke 18:1

Are We There Yet?

I can't tell the story of the "beach miracle" without getting onto the subject of commitment. I think frequently we fail to see answers to our prayers because we are expecting instant answers. We ask for something for a while, nothing happens, we get tired of asking, and we quit. We read an account of a miraculous answer to prayer in scripture, and the story is told so succinctly that we get the impression that the answer came instantly, so we think, *I guess things like that just don't happen anymore.*

For example, when we read the story of the children of Israel crossing the Red Sea, we have a mental image of a Hollywood-style scene of the sea instantly opening up like a cellar door. But Exodus 14:21 says, "Then Moses stretched out his hand over the sea, and all that night the Lord drove the sea back with a strong east wind and turned it into dry land."

The TNT miniseries "Moses" shows this much more accurately than the older Hollywood movie version. At the close of Part I of the miniseries, Moses is shown standing at the edge of the Red Sea, his staff outstretched and the wind whipping his robe as the sun slowly goes down and the Israelites are bedding down for the night. The next night as we tune in again, Part II begins with the sun coming up the next day, and the Israelites awakening to see Moses *still* standing there, and the sea opened up. If it's not necessarily dramatic enough to some people, it does make the story much more believable. No doubt there have been strong winds and out-of-the-ordinary tides on the Red Sea before, so what happened may not have been supernatural, but providential nonetheless. As one preacher explained it, a *miracle* occurs in those rare instances when God breaks the laws of nature. Something is *providential* when what happens can be explained but is nevertheless *timed* to meet a need perfectly. Here the answer to Moses' prayer wasn't the "what" but the "when." A skeptic may explain the natural phenomena that made the Red Sea open up, but not why it *just happened to* open up the night before Israel needed to cross over, and *just happened to* close back in on the pursuing Egyptian army!

Personally, I was more impressed with the character of Moses after watching that scene. We frequently think of him as this out-of-the-ordinary guy with a magic staff he could wave around and make things happen in the blink of an eye, and in some instances he probably did. But you have to appreciate what it took for an ordinary, timid man with a stuttering problem to stand there all night waiting for the Lord to move, especially with the people complaining and blaming him for their troubles. How many of us would have had the perseverance to wait on God all night long under those circumstances?

Josh McDowell tells of a student who came to him close to tears, telling him that one of her professors had told the class that the "Red Sea" was actually the "Reed Sea," or the "Sea of Reeds," and that it was only eight inches deep!

Undaunted, Josh exclaimed, "Praise God! What a miracle! Pharaoh's whole army drowned in eight inches of water!"

Whether Israel walked on dry land through a sea that was usually twenty feet deep, or Pharaoh's army drowned in eight inches of water, God answered Moses' prayers, and Israel got what she needed, *when* she needed it. I think that would be well worth staying up all night to see!

To cite another familiar story, we love to imagine the scene in Joshua

6:20 when the people of Israel shouted and the walls of Jericho came tumbling down. But I'm guessing we don't spend a lot of time visualizing what led up to that moment, because it involved marching around the city in total silence once a day for *six days* and seven times on the seventh day. And frankly, for someone with my short attention span, I think that would get old very quickly. I have to wonder how many people were thinking, *This is crazy! This'll never work!* or *Why are we doing this?* If anyone had been thinking that, they fortunately didn't say so out loud, or who knows what the outcome would have been? (Hence the very wise order for everyone to *keep silent.*) Thank God, they did what they were told, marching and keeping their mouths shut, and their patience paid off. How many of us would be willing to look like fools for seven days without saying a word, waiting for God to come through? For an outcome like that one, I'm thinking now I would!

In Chapter Four we looked at the account of the patriarch Joseph and how long he had to wait for the deliverance he was praying for—literally years. Commitment is all about asking for the right things (and trusting God's timing), having the right priorities, having a relationship with God that makes Him priority, not letting ourselves get distracted, having the right motives, and having faith that is willing to wait—basically everything we have discussed already.

The truth is, God loves obedience, and He loves perseverance. What's worth praying for is worth waiting for. When we ask God for something, we show Him how important it is to us by our commitment, and that commitment shows itself in the form of perseverance.

Think about it: When our children see a toy advertised on TV, they want it. It doesn't really matter what it is; if they see it, they want it. But as Christmas or a birthday approaches, any parent knows that what the child *really* wants is what he *keeps asking* for. If he gets the toy that he asked for just once, chances are that's the one that ends up on the shelf collecting dust.

When it comes to asking God for things, Jesus said, "Ask, and it will be given to you; seek and you will find; knock and the door will be opened to you." (Matthew 7:7) The original verb form meant, literally, "*Keep* asking . . . *keep* seeking . . . *keep* knocking." Are we patient enough to do that?

Do you sense God asking you to pray for something or someone and keep praying and seeking Him until you see Him answer?

The Gazillion Dollar Question

I think in this day and age we are so used to instant solutions, Google answers, and fast food that we have lost the ability to be patient. One has only to watch a half dozen commercials to see that much advertising appeals to the American trademark trait of impatience. (Why spend fifteen minutes saving 15% on insurance when you can do it in half the time?)

I would define patience as the ability either to *refrain* from doing anything but wait, or to continue to *work at* something until you see the results. Depending on your personality, either one can be challenging, to say the least. But there's a question that I think is well worth asking ourselves when we're praying for something and not seeing immediate results::

Would I rather have God's best, years from now, or second best now?

I think a lot of us, if we were honest, would admit that we'd gladly settle for second best, rather than wait or work that long for the best.

I have seen that attitude in myself, and I'm asking God to help me change. What you do with the question is between you and God. I guess the bottom line is, do you want God's best enough to work and/or wait for it?

"It's Not Working!"

Some of us can relate to the embarrassing situation Jesus' disciples encountered when a man came to them for the deliverance of his son who had violent seizures caused by an evil spirit. The disciples tried to cast the spirit out and failed. (Mark 9:17–18) But when Jesus showed up and the father spoke the honest, poignant words that resonate with so many of us—"I do believe; help me overcome my unbelief!" (vs. 24)—the Lord rebuked the demon, and it left.

When Jesus' disciples asked Him why they couldn't drive out the evil spirit, He responded, "This kind can come out only by prayer." (Mark 9:29)

The disciples had been following Jesus for months, and they had seen Him heal and cast out demons. Perhaps they were speaking the very words they had heard Him speak and believed that if they spoke them forcefully enough and with faith that they would have the same results. But they were mistaken.

Note that a few chapters earlier we are told that after feeding the crowds with five loaves and two fish, Jesus had dismissed the crowd and sent His disciples on ahead. "After leaving them, he went up on a mountainside to pray." (Mark 6:46)

Jesus had done something I'm guessing the disciples hadn't; He had spent time alone in prayer. In the book of Acts we are told that after the Resurrection the disciples "*devoted themselves* to the apostles' teaching and to the fellowship, to the breaking of bread and *to prayer.*" (Acts 2:42, italics mine) In the next chapter we read,:

> Peter said [to the crippled beggar] "Silver or gold I do not have, but what I have I give you. In the name of Jesus Christ of Nazareth, walk." Taking him by the right hand, he helped him up, and instantly the man's feet and ankles became strong. He jumped to his feet and began to walk.
>
> Acts 3: 6–8a

Although to the crowds at the temple saw an "instant" healing, we should know by now that what appeared as instant began days, maybe weeks and months before, with Peter's devotion to prayer. (This was the same Peter who could not drive a demon out of a young boy, and who later denied Jesus three times!) Never underestimate the power of arriving "prayed up!"

The Four-Letter Word Some Christians Don't Like

When I read of the disciples' moment of embarrassment and frustration with the demon-possessed boy, I admit I read the footnote with some reluctance. When Jesus responded, "This kind can come out only by prayer," (Mark 9:29) the footnote in the NIV says that some manuscripts say *prayer and fasting*. Most of us have said at one time or another, "I'm going to pray for you." But I'm guessing we don't often (translation: "never"?) say, "I'm going to *fast* and pray." Fasting implies giving up something, and for most of us it's easier to make the effort to do something than *not* to do something—like eating.

How important is that thing you've been praying for? Is it more important than breakfast? More important than chocolate? Facebook? TV?

If you're thinking, *Oh boy, here comes the guilt trip*, please know that fasting is something I have struggled with in various ways over the years.

During my college days I would fast for 24-hour periods and find that I got a lot more done in the way of homework and studies when I wasn't taking time out for meals. I used to joke that the term "fast" was appropriate, because I got things done a lot faster when I wasn't preparing, eating, or cleaning up food. But guess who also wasn't doing much more praying than usual? I may have felt proud of my self-restraint, but I was missing the whole point of a fast, and that was to spend that time in prayer.

On another occasion I spent a day refraining from food, water, gum, TV, and radio. I went out to a sand dune and prayed fervently for the healing of a friend with cancer. She died anyway. So I was confused. (We saw examples of this kind of disappointment in the chapter on priorities.)

Take as another example a wife and mother who is responsible for feeding her family. Refraining from eating doesn't really provide her any more time for uninterrupted prayer than a normal day, since she will still be preparing, serving, and cleaning up after meals. (And being hungry while feeding everyone else doesn't usually help one's attitude any.)

Some individuals have dietary needs that would make a total fast detrimental to their health. Some people get faint if they don't consume enough protein. Here's where our unique situations make it necessary to find what works for us as individuals. Remember, the point of a fast isn't to fit into a certain mold, but to devote more time to drawing near to God. Different kinds of fasts work for different people.

Turn It Off!

My doctor once advised me, "If you're going to fast, fast something besides food!" That's when I discovered that the kind of fast that works best for me (that is, helps me draw near to God and give Him my undivided attention) is a media fast. In some ways this is harder for me than a food fast, but it is the most effective way I know to get my mind off the world and onto God.

I confess I'm somewhat of an addict when it comes to mental stimulation—movies, talk shows, music, conversation—*noise!* When I start my car, my hand reaches for the radio before it reaches for the seatbelt. At the gym I have my headset on and can't imagine working out without the beat of a good song. At home the radio is on nonstop, even when I'm not in the room.

It's not just the radio. Social media has a way of sucking way more time out of my day than it should. What starts as checking my email and Facebook messages can turn into an hour or more of looking at other people's family pictures, reading their cute stories, the latest news, a funny joke, "liking" and commenting on everything, and before I know it half the morning is gone.

During the day, if everything is turned off and the house is quiet, I find myself getting restless. However, when I'm awake at night, that's a different thing. Night is *supposed* to be quiet. (Of course it's also supposed to be sleeping time, but that doesn't always phase this hyperactive mind.) That's probably why I sometimes get a lot more done in the predawn hours of the morning than I do during the day. I should have figured out a long time ago that if I want more productive time with God, I need times when I am giving Him my *full attention—not* listening to someone else talk about Him or sing about Him on Christian radio—time with just Jesus and me. And a media fast helps me more toward that end than being physically hungry ever did.

It's not up to me to recommend a fast to anyone else, especially since it took me most of my adult life to figure out what works for me. But if you are frustrated by lack of quality prayer time, ask God to show you something in your life that you could put on hold—or give up altogether—that would allow you more time with Him. He will reward your sacrifice.

Oops . . .

In speaking of various kinds of fasts, I should probably point out something that you've probably figured out by now, but I'll say it anyway: *Motive matters.* Although we've covered motive in Chapter Three, I can't emphasize enough that it's possible to do things that seem very spiritual and yet miss the mark entirely. The Israelites fell into this trap, and Isaiah nailed them for it. These are God's words, spoken through His prophet:

> "Shout it aloud, do not hold back.
>   Raise your voice like a trumpet.
> Declare to my people their rebellion
>   and to the house of Jacob their sins.
> For day after day they seek me out;
>   they seem eager to know my ways,
> as if they were a nation that does what is right
>   and has not forsaken the commands of its God.
> They ask me for just decisions
>   and seem eager for God to come near them.
> 'Why have we fasted,' they say,
>   and you have not seen it?
> We have humbled ourselves,
>   and you have not noticed?'
> "Yet on the day of your fasting, you do as you please
>   and exploit all your workers.
> Your fasting ends in quarreling and strife,
>   and in striking each other with wicked fists.
> You cannot fast as you do today
>   and expect your voice to be heard on high.
> Is this the kind of fast I have chosen,
>   only a day for a man to humble himself?
> Is it only for bowing one's head like a reed
>   and for lying on sackcloth and ashes?
> Is that what you call a fast,
>   a day acceptable to the LORD?
>
> "Is not this the kind of fasting I have chosen:
>   to loose the chains of injustice
>   and untie the cords of the yoke,
>   to set the oppressed free
>   and break every yoke?

> Is it not to share your food with the hungry
> and to provide the poor wanderer with shelter—
> when you see the naked, to clothe him,
> and not to turn away from your own flesh and blood?"
>
> Isaiah 58:1–7

Oddly, it is possible to be fasting in sackcloth and ashes and still be in *rebellion* (Isaiah's word)! So why were the people fasting? According to Isaiah, they *seemed* to be seeking God. They even go so far as to say (in essence) "Hey God, don't You see us here, depriving ourselves? Don't You see the sackcloth and ashes? Can't You hear our stomachs growling? Aren't You impressed?"

The answer was obviously, "No, not in the least." From Isaiah's description of these people, they must have thought God would only see what they wanted Him to see—their "religious" acts. But from Isaiah's description, there was a lot more going on, and God not only saw it, He was fed up with it. He was sick of not only the people's behavior but their using fasting to try to manipulate Him. Fasting should not be used as a kind of equivalent to a hunger strike. (I admit I never quite understood hunger strikes, anyway.)

It also should not be used to elevate one's spiritual status. If fasting is supposed to humble us, why are so many people proud of doing it?

Jesus reflected God's perspective on true humility, using a parable that no doubt added fuel to the fire of resentment that was growing in the religious establishment of His time. Luke even specified "some who were confident of their own righteousness and looked down on everybody else" (Luke 18:9) as the primary target of a pointed parable:

> "Two men went up to the temple to pray, one a Pharisee and the other a tax collector. The Pharisee stood up and prayed about himself: 'God, I thank you that I am not like other men—robbers, evildoers, adulterers—or even like this tax collector. I fast twice a week and give a tenth of all I get.'

> "But the tax collector stood at a distance. He would not even look up to heaven, but beat his breast and said, 'God, have mercy on me, a sinner!'
>
> "I tell you that this man, rather than the other, went home justified before God. For everyone who exalts himself will be humbled, and he who humbles himself will be exalted."
>
> Luke 18: 2–14

If we're fasting to impress God, to get what we want, or to feel superior to other people, we are doing it for the wrong reason. God is not impressed with our self-control, which is a gift from Him anyway—one of the fruits of His Spirit. (Galatians 5: 22–23) And God doesn't need us to deprive ourselves in order to do what He chooses to do. There are even times when self-denial can be counterproductive . . .

Attitude Is Everything

In my daughter's quest for good health, her diet went through several phases –the vegetarian phase, the "blood-type diet" phase, the gluten-free/dairy-free phase, and my personal pet peeve, the vegan phase. I always tried to show my support by planning meals that took into account whatever were the dietary restrictions at the time. Vegan was by far the most challenging, since not only was meat forbidden but we were also to refrain from fish, eggs, dairy products, or foods that contained any animal products. That meant no gelatin, no ranch dressing for the salads, no sour cream for the baked potatoes, and no butter for the steamed veggies . . . even honey was debatable. Still, ever the devoted mom, I learned all I could about preparing tofu and various high-protein grains, seeds, and nuts.

My husband Marty wasn't thrilled with the recent menus, but one night when he came home from work he was cracking up laughing as he walked through the door. I asked him what in the world was so funny.

He proceeded to tell me how the neighborhood dogs had been on a spree. The street was strewn with Styrofoam meat trays, pizza boxes, KFC buckets, anything remotely related to meat. The dogs had hit every trash can on the block.

Well, almost every one. There in the middle of the chaos stood one lone trash can, upright, neat, and undisturbed. You can probably guess whose trash can that was. (I guess dogs don't go for vegan, either.)

Believe it or not, I see a spiritual application here. There are those of us in the Church who take great pride in what we *don't* do as Christians.

Of course there are things *nobody* should do—theft, murder and other illegal acts.

Then there's a second category, and most Christians at least *try* to refrain from R-rated movies, gambling, excessive use of alcohol, and other socially questionable activities.

Then there are the things that are just generally unhealthy that we try to avoid as good stewards of the bodies God gave us—smoking, gluttony, and the like.

But some people, in the interest of spirituality, have decided to add their own list. These would-be super-saints refrain from *anything* that could be construed as frivolous or unnecessary. (I have known people that I could easily picture praying at the end of the day, ". . . and Lord, if I had any fun today, please forgive me.")

Such extensive sacrifices do require a great deal of self-control—and please don't misunderstand, self-control is a good thing. But in denying ourselves anything and everything that gives us pleasure, are we still presenting the gospel to the world in an inviting way? When people see us, do they see the joy of the Lord, or do they see people who never laugh, rarely smile, tend to judge everybody else, and generally lead drab, unexciting lives? In other words, are they going to *want* what we have?

Christians should be the happiest people on the planet! Just think—we have *grace*. The Lord of everything loves us enough to die for us. He's the greatest, most creative mind in the universe, and we get to spend eternity with Him. He's the inventor of joy and laughter. He's with us every moment of every day, to love us, protect us, encourage us, guide us, and meet our every need. He even surprises us with little blessings when we least expect them. The Christian life is a joyous serendipity, and it should resemble one unending celebration!

In other words, it should be *fun*. (There. I said it.)

If our lives reflect that kind of joy, we won't have to go about looking for converts, they'll be coming to *us*, wanting what we have.

So wear make-up, or don't wear makeup. Dance, or don't dance. But don't be so concerned with winning first prize for self-denial. Like our trash can, you may be the only one left standing when it's all over, but what will you have missed? The Christian life is an adventure. So we might make some mistakes along the way—that's what grace is there for. Much better to fall down occasionally than to reach the end of one's life never having taken a risk for the kingdom of God for fear of tarnishing our halos. Jesus came to give us "life in abundance." Let's enjoy it!

And let's see how many people are attracted to Him because of our joy.

So, what am I saying here? Our prayers (and our joy) can be hindered not only by our lack of commitment, but by our commitment to the wrong things, for the wrong reasons. This goes back to two barriers we've already discussed: misdirected attention (Our focus should be on the LORD, not on any specific discipline.) and motive (We should use self-discipline as a means to *give* to God, not to *get* something from Him or to take pride in ourselves.)

One Final Note

Know the difference between commitment and stubbornness. No matter how persistent we are, God is still God, and His answer may still be "no." And even though we may not be seeing the answers *we* want, *when* we want, that doesn't mean we can't still wait in joyful expectation, knowing that God knows far more than we do, and when His answer is "no," that's really the best answer. As I used to tell my children, He will give us either what we asked for, or something better!

And when we have that attitude, we will be able to rejoice in whatever His answer is, and to say that not only was it worth every minute of waiting, but the waiting itself wasn't all that bad.

Chapter Eight

BARRIER

#8

DISOBEDIENCE (SIN)

If I had cherished sin in my heart,
The Lord would not have listened.
Psalm 66:18

In the last chapter we read that in Isaiah's time people were fasting and going through religious rituals and wondering why God seemingly wasn't hearing them. And Isaiah made it very clear that not only was their shallow fasting inadequate, but their sins were not going unnoticed.

Malachi also dealt with a people whose sins had separated them from God. These sins included bringing blind, crippled, or diseased animals to sacrifice on the altar instead of the unblemished sacrifices that they should have offered (Malachi 1: 7, 8, 14), not keeping their vows, half-hearted worship (1: 13, 2: 2), false teaching (2: 7, 8), partiality (2: 9), marital unfaithfulness (2:13–15), divorce (2: 16), taking God's grace for granted (2: 17) and a string of other sins—sorcery, adultery, perjury, defrauding, oppression of widows and orphans, and depriving aliens of justice. (3: 5)

And the people's response was, basically. "Who? *Us*?"

When Malachi accuses them of robbing God, they ask "How?" and he tells them in failing to tithe. When Malachi tells them they have said harsh things against God, they want to know, "What?" And Malachi points to their grumbling against the LORD, calling evil "good" and good "evil." The book of Malachi is only four chapters long, and most of it is a dialogue between God (speaking through Malachi) and the people. It's well worth reading, especially if there's any doubt that sins—of commission or omission—can affect our relationship with God, and hence, our prayers. And the way to deal with sin is not just to sweep it under the rug.

The Big Cover-up

In 1976 Marty and I moved to a house in the woods near a tiny town in Michigan. Knowing there was wildlife all around, I was always on the lookout for deer, foxes, raccoons—anything interesting (except skunks. That I suppose I could pass up, thank you.).

After a while I was disappointed by the lack of sightings, so I began tossing food scraps into our yard every night after dinner, hoping to spot a hungry critter. Every morning the scraps had disappeared, but I was never able to spot a single creature, and usually the snow had been falling lightly but steadily all night enough to cover up any tracks.

Since I am not the type of person who can stare at nature all winter, I got involved with the local high school students. Before I knew it a Christian youth group made up of about a dozen kids was meeting in my living room every week. By March they wanted to share their faith with their friends from school, so we planned a special night of outreach—fondue, music, and a message at the end. The students invited all their friends and posted announcements about it at school.

Finally the big day arrived, and while the students were at school I was busy getting everything ready. I bought the ingredients and got out the equipment for the fondue and cleaned the house till it sparkled. I wanted everything to be *perfect.*

As the time for the party approached I was feeling pretty satisfied with myself, when I realized I was missing one ingredient for the fondue. *No big deal,* I thought, as I headed out the door for a quick run into town. Suddenly I froze in horror.

That day had been unseasonably warm, and the snow that had been accumulating all winter was fast melting away. And throughout the yard, everywhere I looked was . . .

GARBAGE!

Apple cores, potato peelings, eggshells, bread crusts, broccoli stems, you name it. All over the yard. The animals hadn't eaten it. It had just been covered up every night by the steadily falling snow!

So much for perfection.

Have you ever had one of those moments? Things you thought no one would ever know about—things maybe *you* didn't even know about—are suddenly out in the open for all to see?

The Bible says a day like that will come, when every moment of bad judgment, wrong words, thoughts, motives, and deeds will be brought to light—and judged by a holy God. How scary is that, especially since we have all made more bad decisions than we can count? "Who can endure the day of his coming?" (Malachi 3: 2a)

If having company see your house surrounded in garbage is embarassing, imagine having the whole universe see . . . (You fill in the blanks.)

That night in 1977 I was scrambling to clean up my yard, but it will take much more than a rake and a garbage bag to undo a lifetime of sins and mistakes.

Well, there's good news: it has been done! When Jesus Christ was nailed to that cross 2000 years ago, He was paying the penalty for every bad decision you and I have ever made. In fact, when He cried "It is finished!" He was declaring, literally, "Paid in full."

If we believe that His death has paid for our sins, why on earth would we try to cover them up?

> If we claim to be without sin, we deceive ourselves, and the truth is not in us. If we confess our sins, he is faithful and just and will forgive us our sins and purify us from all unrighteousness.
>
> I John 1:8–9

If confessing our sins can mean the slate is clean, why would we *not* confess? If repentance means that when God looks at you, He sees not the garbage in your life but a soul washed clean, why would we want to hang onto the thing that separates us from Him?

> He who conceals his sins does not prosper,
>
> but whoever confesses and renounces them finds mercy.
>
> Proverbs 28: 13

Is there a mess in your life that you're hiding? If so, are you going to keep trying to cover it up, or will you confess your mess and ask the Lord for His help?

I recommend the latter.

Oh . . . that . . .

Whether you realize it or not, prayer is a dialogue between you and God. His voice may not be audible like that of a human friend, but know that He does have a great deal to say.

Has this ever happened to you? You've been praying and feeling as though your prayers were bouncing off the ceiling, and suddenly a memory pops into your mind of something you did or said, or something you failed to do or say that you knew was not pleasing to God? This could well be God's unspoken answer to your unspoken question, specifically, "Why don't I feel my prayer is getting through?"

Jesus was well aware that we humans are repeatedly in need of forgiveness. In the brief model prayer He taught His disciples, He included the much-needed request to "forgive us our debts, as we forgive our debtors." It's not that God expects us to be perfect. He knows we aren't, and that there are certain weaknesses in each of us that we struggle with. In fact, there are certain things I have confessed to God again and again, until I thought He surely must be sick of forgiving me for *that*. After all, I've done that wrong thing (or failed to do the right thing) so many times . . .

Have you ever wondered if there's a point where He says, "That's it! That was your last chance! I'm not forgiving you anymore!"? I know I have, or I used to, but I have found great comfort and encouragement in Psalms, because whatever my feelings are, I can know that I'm not the only one. And when it comes to expressing the overwhelming conviction of sin and guilt, the best example is Psalm 51.

If It Can Happen To *Him* . . .

Psalm 51 was written by David after Nathan confronted him about his affair with Bathsheba and the murder of her husband as part of the cover-up—serious stuff. (If you are unfamiliar with this story, you can read all about it in 2 Samuel 11.)

This was not an "Oh-no-I-just-sinned!" moment for David. He had gone at least nine months without confessing what he had done as sin, and although there were no doubt people under him who knew all about it, no one had yet shown the courage to confront the king.

Only after Bathsheba had borne David a son did the Lord send the prophet Nathan to the king. He drew David in with a heart-wrenching story of a wealthy man with many sheep, who took and killed the one little lamb that a poor man had. Having once been a shepherd, David burned with anger and declared that the rich man deserved to die, prompting Nathan's famous words: "You are the man!" (2 Samuel 12:7b)

Think of it! David, a "man after God's own heart," was capable of adultery and murder! But even such a horrendous crime, covered up for nearly a year, could be forgiven, *if* David confessed and repented.

If such a spiritual giant as David could have fallen so low, we should never think that we won't have sins to confess and ask forgiveness for.

David had gained nothing from trying to hide his sin. Verse 3 of Psalm 51 says, "For I know my transgressions, and my sin is *always* before me." (Italics mine) He had known God, and the sin he tried to forget had no doubt been eating at him every day, whether he was consciously aware of it or not. In verse 12, he begs God, "Restore to me the joy of your salvation." Most of us can testify that when something is on our conscience, it drains away whatever joy we once had.

Whether the sin is murder, adultery, or gossip, sin is sin, and I for one can identify with David's anguish as he pleads with the Lord to "Wash away all my iniquity and cleanse me from my sin." (Psalm 51:2)

So why do we so often procrastinate when it comes to confessing our sins and repenting? Do we think we can "fix it" ourselves?

Do we seriously think God won't know about it if we don't tell Him?

Do we think God's got bigger things to think about, like wars and epidemics, so we don't want to bother God with our little issues?

Do we think, "It's not that big a deal, I won't do it again," . . . and then we do it again?

Are we waiting, thinking eventually it won't be a big deal, because it will have been such a long time that everyone will have forgotten, even God—as if sin had an expiration date or a statute of limitations?

Are we just too ashamed to admit that we blew it?

Are we busy trying to figure out a way to blame someone *else*?

Are we trying to justify what we did by looking at the way "all things work together for good . . ."?

If all that sounded like a lot of work to you, that's because *it is!* Much more work than just coming to God and confessing, "Lord, I've sinned," or even, "Lord, I blew it—*again*." (It's not as if He doesn't know about it anyway.) Humbling yourself may sting at first, but the relief of being forgiven is well worth it—and much less trouble than avoiding it day after day.

Besides, every day that goes by with sin in your heart is a day that you are alienated from the God that can answer your prayers. Don't you want to clear the way for Him to work in your life?

"But I like it . . ."

Of course, there's a question that wasn't included in the list that's in a whole different category: Are you not confessing a sin because you are still doing it, you *like* what you're doing, and you have no intention of stopping? If so, you have a more serious problem.

Or for that matter, are you confessing and *still* have no intention of stopping? Are you thinking, *I can always "repent" again.*?

If the answer to either of those questions is "yes," you need to reexamine your relationship with Christ. Anyone who is fully aware of what He has already done for us does not take His grace for granted. Anyone preferring the pleasure of sin to Christ is practicing *idolatry.*

There is more to true repentance than saying "I'm sorry." We've all known what it's like to have someone say "sorry" that seemed to just want to get it over with and who sounded as if he had neither any idea how much pain he had caused nor any intention of stopping the behavior. The word "repent" means, literally, to *turn around and go in the other direction.*

This may present a problem if you are "hooked" on the sin, or if a seed of selfish rebellion is still present. You may not want to stop the behavior that is so offensive to God, but if you *want* to want to, ask Him to deal with your heart, and He will. Be open to the possibility that He may send you to a mature fellow Christian for help. Although God can and wants to deliver you from destructive habits, He often chooses to do it through a brother or sister, especially one who is older, wiser, and more experienced. That is what the Body of Christ is all about. Be humble enough to accept counsel!

Even if your heart's desire is to live the way God wants you to, if your conscience is tender, you might be tormented by the thought, "If I tell God I'm sorry and do this *again*, I'm *really* in big trouble then!" Don't let Satan use this as an excuse to avoid bringing it up in the first place.

This line of thinking seriously underestimates God's grace.

> ". . . he knows how we are formed,
> he remembers that we are dust."
> Psalm 103:14

Know that God understands your struggle, and He will not expect anything from you beyond what you can do. Now, He may ask more from you than *you think* you can do, but that's because you may be forgetting that He's there to help, and He's provided people in your life to help, as well. We don't have to promise never to sin again, but we should commit to *trying* not to sin, asking for His help when we struggle, and asking His forgiveness when we fail. He expects no more from us. (Aren't you glad?)

> The LORD is compassionate and gracious,
> slow to anger, abounding in love.
> He will not always accuse,
> nor will he harbor his anger forever;
> he does not treat us as our sins deserve
> or repay us according to our iniquities.
> For as high as the heavens are above the earth,

so great is his love for those who fear him;
as far as the east is from the west,
so far has he removed our transgressions from us.
As a father has compassion on his children,
So the LORD has compassion on those who fear him;
for he knows how we are formed,
he remembers that we are dust.

Psalm 103:8–14

There was a time in my life when I would read this psalm almost every day. I needed the reassurance that God was not like people, who lose patience after a while. I clung to this scripture like a lifeline, and it helped me through the struggle.

One Man's Sin

Not only can someone's willful sin place a barrier on that person's prayers, but it can affect a whole congregation. A sad example is in the book of Joshua, where one of the Bible's most glowing examples of the rewards of obedience—the fall of Jericho—is followed by an excruciating example of how one man's disobedience brought condemnation on the whole camp.

Remember, the Israelites obeyed God, marching silently around the city thirteen times. After circling the city for the final time and giving a shout, they watched the walls come down, and Jericho was theirs. The high point of the story is in Joshua 6: 16, as "Joshua commanded the people, 'Shout! For the LORD has given you the city!" It would be nice if the story ended there, but in the midst of their victory, Joshua had a stern warning for the people:

> "But keep away from the devoted things, so that you will not bring about your own destruction by taking any of them. Otherwise you will make the camp of Israel liable to destruction and bring trouble on it."
>
> Joshua 6:18

The warning couldn't have been more explicit. Every Israelite knew that "devoted" things were to be given over to the LORD—in other words, totally destroyed. But one man couldn't resist taking something for himself, and the consequences were not manifested until the next battle.

After such an impressive triumph over Jericho, Israel was stunned when an attack on the tiny city of Ai resulted in humiliation. The men of Ai routed the Israelites, killing thirty-six of them.

Joshua and the elders tore their clothes and prostrated themselves before the LORD until evening, seeking an explanation of what had gone wrong.

> The LORD said to Joshua, "Stand up! What are you doing down on your face? Israel has sinned; they have violated my covenant, which I commanded them to keep. They have taken some of the devoted things; they have stolen, they have lied, they have put them with their own possessions. That is why the Israelites cannot stand against their enemies; they turn their backs and run, because they have been made liable to destruction. I will not be with you anymore unless you destroy whatever among you is devoted to destruction."
>
> Joshua 7: 10–12

Notice that although it was just one man who stole something, God said "Israel has sinned."

After having all the tribes present themselves, God singled out the tribe of Judah. When the clans of Judah presented themselves, God singled out the Zerahites. When the families of the Zerahites came forward, the family of Zimri was taken. (Can you imagine the emotions of the guilty man as God narrowed down the suspects?)

Finally, man by man, they came forward, and God singled out Achan.

> Achan replied, "It is true! I have sinned against the Lord, the God of Israel. This is what I have done: When I saw in the plunder a beautiful robe from Babylonia, two hundred shekels of silver and a wedge of gold weighing fifty shekels, I coveted them and took them. They are hidden in the ground inside my tent, with the silver underneath."
>
> Joshua 7: 20–21

I'm not sure why Achan gave the specifics. Did it really matter exactly *what* he took? Did he think anyone would sympathize with him? Of course the treasures were tempting, but I doubt Achan got any sympathy, especially from the relatives of the thirty-six men who had been killed as a result of his disobedience. The Bible says that "all Israel" stoned him and his children and burned them and everything Achan had owned (vs. 25) and buried them under a pile of rocks.

Here's another question to ponder: Just what did Achan plan to do with what he took for himself? Did he plan to wear the Babylonian robe? ("Hey, Achan, nice robe! Where's you get it?" . . . "Well, remember when we conquered Jericho and Joshua told us not to take any of their stuff?" . . .) And what would he have done with the gold and silver? Cash it in? Where?

I'm guessing Achan wasn't really thinking that far ahead. If he had, he might have been much wiser.

It's embarrassing how often we are tempted to do something for no particular reason. Like a compulsive shopper after purchasing things that turn out to be useless,

Aachen's only explanation was, "I coveted them and took them."

Here's some advice for anyone who is tempted: Instead of setting your focus on the satisfaction of having what you want, fast-forward your imagination to the likely scenario *after* the sin has been exposed. (And before you tell me, "It won't," hear me out.) For example, suppose you are married yet find yourself attracted to someone besides your spouse. If you feel your mind taken over by the attraction, instead of letting the enemy lure your mind with fantasies of how romantic it would be to be with that person, deliberately focus your thoughts to the next day. What would it feel like to wake up in the wrong bed? How would you explain to your children why you didn't come home last night? How do you explain to the Church why your marriage is failing? . . . You get the idea. These fantasies aren't nearly as fun as what the enemy wants you to focus on, but they will go a long way in thwarting the attack from the "immediate gratification" demons and will help you get back on track.

You didn't just see that . . .

Besides the momentary, illogical coveting of something one neither needs nor can use, another reason for the "secret sin" issue is the absurd notion (conscious or unconscious) that we could keep anything secret from an all-knowing God. Or that He knows about it, but He's not going to tell anybody. (Ask David how that worked out for him.)

Jeremiah had some choice words for the people of Israel in his time, who were committing gross sins and believing they could get away with these things because they still had the Temple, as though God were some senile grandfather who didn't have a clue what was going on.

> "Will you steal and murder, commit adultery and perjury, burn incense to Baal and follow other gods you have not known, and then come and stand before me in this house, which bears my Name, and say, 'We are safe'—safe to do all these detestable things? Has this house, which bears my Name, become a den of robbers to you? But I have been watching!" declares the LORD.
>
> Jeremiah 7: 9–11

Israel should have known, and we should know, there is nothing hidden from God. Jesus said:

> "There is nothing concealed that will not be disclosed, or hidden that will not be made known. What you have said in the dark will be heard in the daylight, and what you have whispered in the ear in the inner rooms will be proclaimed from the roofs."
>
> Luke 12:2–3

The notion of "secret sin" is a lie of the enemy to get us to keep sinning, to keep us separated from God, instead of confessing and renouncing our sins so our fellowship with our Father is restored—and so our prayers can be effective again.

Assume you'll get caught.

When I taught English literature and we studied Shakespeare's *Macbeth*, there was always a discussion when we came to the scene where Lady Macbeth persuades her husband to kill the king. (Act I, scene 5) Macbeth says, in essence, "What if we get caught?"

Her response, in essence, is, "We *won't* get caught!"

I point out to the students that this scene has been repeated in *countless* books, plays, movies, and TV shows: One criminal always says, "What if we get caught?" and the other *always* says, "We won't get caught." (You've probably heard or read many of them.)

And guess what. Invariably, *they get caught.*

My advice for my students has always been, "Assume you'll get caught." To make sure they get it, I have them repeat it. It was amazing how often that mantra came up as we studied other literature. It may take time, but if the story is at all realistic, the characters *always* get caught! The tragedy is, usually the revelation comes after irreversible disaster, for an individual, a family, a church, or a nation.

Another Kind of Sin

It's possible that we can be free of the kinds of actions that people usually think of when hearing the word "sin," and yet still be out of God's will. James, in his short but practical letter, nailed it succinctly: "Anyone, then, who knows the good he ought to do and doesn't do it, sins." (James 4: 17) He was referring, of course, to what we call the "sin of omission."

When people pray the Lord's Prayer, some say, "Forgive us our trespasses as we forgive those who trespass against us." Some say "Forgive us our debts, as we forgive our debtors." Personally I prefer the term "debts" to "trespasses," not only because that was the version I was brought up with, but because I know that many of my sins are sins of *omission*—lost opportunities—so I am "indebted" to God not only in owing Him an apology for things I've done, but also owing Him the obedience I have so often failed to give Him.

"If Only . . .!"

Contrary to some people's image of God as an angry old man waiting to pound anyone that displeases Him, the God of both the Old and New Testaments is more eager to bless us than we are to be blessed.

Psalm 81 contains a warning from God to Israel, followed by a cry of frustration at their inability to receive His blessings in their disobedient state.

> "If my people would but listen to me,
>   if Israel would follow my ways,
> how quickly would I subdue their enemies
>   and turn my hand against their foes!
> Those who hate the LORD would cringe before him,
>   and their punishment would last forever.
> But you would be fed with the finest of wheat;
>   with honey from the rock I would satisfy you."
>
> Psalm 81: 13–16

When Jesus echoed this sentiment, He sounded more like a sad father when he cried,

> "O Jerusalem, Jerusalem, you who kill prophets and stone those sent to you, how often I have longed to gather your children together, as a hen gathers her chicks under her wings, but you were not willing."
>
> Matthew 23: 37

Our sin grieves God, not just because it hurts Him, but because it hurts *us*, and because He loves us and wants better things for us. Too often we prefer the fleeting pleasure of sin to God's eternal love and blessing.

(Nobody said we were smart.)

One Last Reminder

Not only does sin affect our prayers and our lives, but as we saw with Achan, sin can affect the whole congregation. Think of some of the goals of your church. Is any sinful pleasure worth jeopardizing the birth of a new ministry? Is any personal satisfaction worth more than an expanded facility to accommodate an ever-growing flock? Does any pleasure outweigh the salvation of loved ones? Can rebellion compete with r*evival?*

In other words, what are you putting at risk to continue in your sin?

Let's keep short accounts with God, ask Him to cleanse us daily of any and all sin, hold one another accountable, and watch what He can do with a church that truly honors Him with obedience.

Chapter Nine

BARRIER #9

UNFORGIVENESS

"I tell you the truth, if anyone says to this mountain, 'Go, throw yourself into the sea,' and does not doubt in his heart but believes that what he says will happen, it will be done for him. Therefore I tell you, whatever you ask for in prayer, believe that you have received it, and it will be yours. And when you stand praying, if you hold anything against anyone, forgive him, so that your Father in heaven may forgive you your sins."

Mark 11: 23–26

In a variation on the scenario in the last chapter, imagine you've been praying and feeling as if your prayers are hitting the ceiling. (This happens a lot, doesn't it?) Suddenly a seemingly random memory invades your mind, but this time it isn't something that you did, it's something that was done to you. And whether it was yesterday or twenty years ago, the thought makes you angry. As in the other scenario, God is speaking to you, and you need to listen. But this time He isn't asking you to confess, He's asking you to forgive, which may be even harder.

When you know you've sinned, your sense of right and wrong makes you feel guilty, at least if you truly love the Lord. Confession may be difficult, but you know it's needed, and it's the right thing to do.

But when someone has wronged *you*, you may feel justified to hold onto your anger, especially if you have always treated that person well, if that person hurt you deliberately, or if that person has never apologized. We can think of all kinds of justifications for staying mad, but staying mad will only make us sick.

Sick? Yes, *sick*. It is true what has been said so often, that holding onto anger is like drinking poison and waiting for the other person to die. If you have ever lain awake nights reliving an unpleasant experience and thinking up clever, cutting things to say to or about the perpetrator, while the offender is probably sleeping soundly, possibly unaware or not remembering what he's done to you, then you know that such an attitude is not a healthy thing. Even more damaging is the way it blocks your prayers, holds you back from following God's call for your life, and ultimately drives a wedge between you and God.

If there's something you're holding onto now that's eating at your soul, and if you are holding onto that thing, your prayers are being hindered!

I'm not saying that you haven't had bad things happen. There's a good chance you've been through more suffering than I can ever imagine, and what those people did to you was inexcusable. You may never heal from the wounds they inflicted. So how can you forgive and go on as if those things never happened?

The bad news is, you can't.

The good news is, *He can*.

You may think it's impossible to forgive people who haven't apologized, because as long as they're unrepentant, how will they be forgiven? Isn't that a condition for being forgiven?

But for you to give that person over to Him, Jesus didn't give conditions, He just said, "Forgive."

The bad news is, you usually won't *feel* like forgiving.

The good news is, you don't *have to* feel like it.

Isn't it interesting how the whole "Go with what you know, not with how you feel" thing comes back again and again? Obedience has very little to do with emotions, it has everything to do with the will.

But if you decide to forgive someone and still have ill feelings toward them, have you really forgiven?

The surprising answer is, *Yes*, if you have deliberately, willfully given it to God. He knows how you feel, and although He doesn't command you to feel anything, He will help heal those bad emotions. Again, it's an act of faith on your part—giving it to Him *before* you see Him heal you.

Help!

When I was about to graduate from college, I woke up one morning with my mind in turmoil. For some reason my thoughts were being invaded by hoards of bad memories. It seemed that I was remembering every person who had ever hurt me in any way.

Where did all this come from? I wondered as I tried to fight off the ill will that was overwhelming me. I knew that holding onto bitter memories of others was not acceptable to God, so for a while I tried to talk myself out of my bad feelings.

That person didn't really hurt me that badly . . . Then why are you obsessing about it ten years later?

That person didn't hurt me on purpose . . . oh yeah, I guess he did.

Well, she didn't know she hurt me . . . She did after you told her, and she still didn't apologize. . . .

Well, it didn't really matter, it wasn't that important. Are you serious? You lost a friend!

I probably deserved it . . . Shoot, now I have to try to forgive myself.

It seemed the more I wrestled with the things in my mind, the more I was only digging myself a deeper hole, until finally I did the sensible thing and turned to God.

"Lord, I need Your help!" In spite of the bitter atmosphere, I knew by faith that He was listening. "I'm trying to think of reasons to forgive these people, and I can't do it. They don't deserve to be forgiven."

The Still, Small Voice spoke to my heart. *You're right, they don't.* I was surprised and wondered whether I was just hearing my own thoughts, but then Still Small Voice said, *How about forgiving them because I'm asking you to?*

I lay there as the early morning sun flooded the room and consciously reminded myself of what Jesus had done for me—created me, blessed me, forgiven me, healed me, . . . suffered unimaginable torture and died for me. I closed my eyes and pictured my Beloved on the cross—the cross He didn't have to accept but did, for me.

"Yes. I can do it for You. But I'll need Your help." I didn't "hear" anything after that, but I didn't need to. I already knew that if I wanted to do His will, He was more than willing to help.

To this day I don't remember all the things that had plagued my mind that morning, nor do I want to. Sometimes forgetfulness is a wonderful thing.

A Clean Scar

It has been said that if you haven't forgotten, you can't have forgiven. But some things are impossible to forget. For example, I remember a woman who was on a Christian talk show who had been blinded and robbed. God had done the impossible and empowered her to forgive the criminals for what they had done to her. However, He had not given her a miraculous physical healing. Obviously there was no way she could forget she was blind. But her smile radiated the joy of the Lord, and it was plain that she was not trapped in a prison of bitterness.

She explained that some things are impossible to forget, but if you have forgiven, rather than being a festering wound, that thing is a clean scar.

Turning the Negative Around

I know of countless Christians whose past hurts have been redeemed and used as part of their ministry. Their experiences have opened doors of trust to minister to people who are going through the same struggles, and their stories have given encouragement to others who desperately need hope.

Forgiveness is liberating. Again, it involves acting *before* the reward. I have gone out of my way to do or say something kind to someone instead of revenge, and after a pleasant visit have gone away with a weight lifted from my heart, feeling overwhelmingly blessed. Maybe it's a rebellious streak in me, but there's something fun about doing something positive that's completely counterintuitive. Maybe it's imagining how it frustrates the enemy that makes me smile.

Or maybe it's just knowing that it makes Jesus smile.

If you think you just can't do it, think of it this way: If certain people have evil motives and want to stir up trouble, you will frustrate them by being kind and forgiving, pleasant and happy. (It can be fun to watch the shocked looks on their faces, too.) On the other hand, if they didn't mean to hurt you—there's nothing to forgive.

Even the little annoyances can be a hindrance to prayer because of the way they chip away at your attitude. Get in the habit of recognizing them and giving them to the Lord, too. That jerk that cut you off on the ride home, the jerk going through the express line with 35 items, . . . well, you get the idea. Did you know that God loves each of them, too? How do I know? I've been one of them.

That Passenger

*Why do people insist on **carrying** their bags on board?*

I was standing in line to board the flight to St. Louis and marveling at people's willingness to lug heavy (and large enough to be questionable) bags on board, when I never hesitated to check mine.

OK, I admit my real concern was not for other people's convenience. I was stressing because I was one of the few passengers in boarding group "C," and I was carrying one of my most precious possessions—a $1,000 12-string guitar, and I was *not* going to turn that delicate instrument over to baggage handlers to be thrown around like a sack of potatoes.

It was highly unusual for me to be in this position. Ordinarily I would make sure I was among the first in line, so I could safely stow my "baby" in the overhead compartment, which was always *plenty* big to hold it, no matter what the flight attendants might tell you. I also usually made sure I was on the airline that never gave me a problem about the guitar, the ones I have actually known to go *out of their way* to accommodate me, hence my loyalty to (Shall I name the company?).

But this time I had received the call less than twelve hours before: my father was dying, and I had better get there soon if I wanted to say good-bye. Ignoring the airline company name, I had grabbed the first flight available and thrown together the essentials. First on the list: my guitar, so I could possibly play and sing Dad the songs he loved one more time . . .

"You're going to have to check that." I can't say I was surprised to hear the order, but I was not about to comply.

"Can you *guarantee* that it will arrive in St. Louis undamaged?"

"No," came the predictable answer.

"If it's damaged, would the airline replace it?" (I knew this script.)

"No." *Surprise, surprise.*

"Then I'm not checking it."

I should explain that I don't usually behave this way. I am the one who tries to get along with *everyone*. I'm compliant to a fault, my friends tell me. But when it involved my father's leaving this world and my chance to give him a few more minutes of pleasure . . . well, push had definitely come to shove.

We made our way to the back of the plane, where the irritated attendant showed me that every last bin was stuffed with other people's junk, and there was no room. I spotted one compartment that had not been open and asked, "What about that one?"

The attendant opened the bin to show me that it was filled with pillows.

"Perfect. I'll take it."

By this time a second attendant had shown up to find out what (or who) was the cause of the delay. For the first time I looked around and noticed all eyes on me, and from the facial expressions, I realized with horror that I had become "*that* passenger!"

The first flight attendant started to refuse my "request," but the second one, no doubt just wanting to get going, yanked pillows out of the compartment, flinging them onto the floor until there was room for the guitar. He stuffed it in, buried it in the pillows, slammed the bin shut, and sternly ordered me to take the last seat, which was right across the aisle: the seat next to the sky marshal. (I don't remember how I knew that. Either the attendants mentioned it—lest I try to cause more trouble—or I just happened to notice that he was the only one visibly carrying a weapon.)

The sky marshal stepped into the aisle so I could take the window seat (i.e., be securely confined for the flight). I meekly buckled myself in and stared out the window, not wanting to make eye contact with anyone.

As we took off, the humiliation soon gave way to sadness as a thousand memories tumbled through my mind. Mental images were bittersweet: the view of a parade from the shoulders of a tall, strong man; laughing around the dinner table at his antics and the playful scolding of my mother; the way he always built the traditional fire in the fireplace on Christmas day; being tossed into the air in the pool so I could perform a full flip before splashing into the clear water, only to be scooped up again in his big arms. I remembered the silly songs he'd make up on the spot (Paul McCartney he was not.) and the awesome flying saucer runs he'd build out of the deep snowdrifts in our back yard. I remembered snuggling in his lap, and his always asking if I had any kisses left. I remember the valuable lessons he'd taught me about finances: saving, spending, and investing money. (And I'd thought we were just playing Monopoly.)

I had flashbacks of smiling pictures of the two of us at my birthdays, graduation, and moments before he walked me down the aisle to give me away. Visions of him with his grandchildren brought a wistful smile to my face, as I remembered his delight at having an excuse to be "silly" again.

The silliness had come in handy when he was diagnosed with Alzheimer's. After the first stressful months of realizing that he was losing his ability to retain things, he finally had slipped into the mindset of a little child—a *sweet* little child, who quickly became everyone's favorite at the nursing home. I remember the day he declared, "Ann! I remembered what it was I forgot to do! I forgot to grow up!" And I remembered my impatience melting away as I hugged him, realizing I still loved him, just the way he was.

I recalled the look of confusion and devastation on his face when my mother passed away, like a little lost puppy. And my mind flashed back to the last time my sister and I had seen him. It had been just a couple of weeks earlier. We had planned a party for him for his ninetieth birthday, and his nieces, nephews, and a few old friends had joined us for the festivities. After almost two hours of "partying," Dad had been exhausted, and as we all said goodbye, half asleep in his recliner, he had mumbled, "I love you so much . . . Wherever you are . . . wherever I am . . . I will *always* love you . . ." I remembered looking at my sister and knowing we were both wondering the same thing: *Was he saying goodbye?*

As the plane descended, I felt the knot in my stomach come back, as I wondered if my father would still be alive when I got there.

"It looks like we're arriving right on time." It took a moment for me to realize that the sky marshal was making a last-minute attempt at conversation.

"I sure hope so," I replied, and I wondered if he noticed the catch in my voice. There was a long pause, and I felt the need to explain myself.

"I got the call late last night. My father's dying." I turned to him and our eyes met, but he didn't say anything more. What else was there to say? I felt myself blush, thinking of my earlier behavior. Glancing at the overhead bin across the aisle, I explained with a shrug, "He likes to hear me sing." I turned back to the window, so he wouldn't see the tears spill over, and there was no more conversation after that, just a long, awkward silence as we waited for the plane to land.

It seemed like forever before the announcement came for us to start to deplane. When it was our turn to leave, I was surprised to see the sky marshal jump out of his seat and fetch my guitar for me. As he handed it to me, he said kindly, "I hope you get to sing to your father."

I thanked him. I don't know if my words were audible, but I think he understood. As I made my way down the aisle and off the plane, I still didn't make eye contact with anyone; I was painfully aware that I was probably still seen as "*that* passenger." But it felt good to know that there was at least one person on that plane that understood why I had acted the way I did.

So, why am I sharing this story? I'm pretty sure all of us at one time or another have encountered "*that* passenger." (Or "*that* customer," or "*that* driver.") We have probably all had the same reaction as everybody else—irritation, rolling our eyes, maybe even a snide remark or two, with those around us in complete agreement. I know I have. I just hope that next time I encounter someone behaving in a way I think is inappropriate and inexcusable, I will remind myself that "*that* person" probably has a story. And I doubt that anyone's story is that they woke up that morning and said "I think I'll be a jerk today."

How to stand out

We often wonder, "How can we, as Christians, express the love of Christ in a way that people will really notice?" I have a radical suggestion: Next time you see one of "*those* people," the moment you recognize your initial irritation, make a point of being kind to that person, even if—*especially* if—everyone else is totally exasperated. I guarantee that you will make an impression. If not on the crowd, it will definitely affect the person who's acting like a jerk. (Now you know how I know.) And pray for that person. He or she may not be an "enemy" necessarily, but if we get in the habit of forgiving and praying past the small offenses, it could make it easier to forgive the big sins.

Another Kind of Letting Go

I mentioned in the last chapter that I tend to use the words "debts" and "debtors" in the Lord's Prayer because of my frequent failure to do the right thing—my "sins of omission." This expression of repentance and forgiveness also reminds me to let go of the people who are "indebted" to me, who may have failed to do what I expected of them. They may not have been there when I needed them, although I had been there for them. I may have experienced trouble that they could have rescued me from, but whether from apathy or ignorance, they hadn't done so.

They may never have thanked me for something I had done for them, or shown what I would consider adequate appreciation. In these cases, as with blatant sins against me, I need to *let it go*.

(Besides, if I was keeping score, I wasn't really giving, was I?)

Forgiveness and Miracles

As I hope you know by now, God wants to do wonderful, amazing, beautiful, even miraculous things in our lives. What is the biggest thing you're praying for—the healing of a marriage, the salvation of a loved one, the safety of someone in harm's way? Know that God wants the best for you and for every person you are praying for. If you are holding on to bitterness over some offense, big or small, it isn't just wasted energy, it's hindering your prayers. Jesus' admonition to forgive comes right after telling His disciples that their faith can move mountains! What is the mountain in your life that God wants to move for you? Whatever grudge you're holding, is it really worth forfeiting God's blessing? Is what you're mad about more important than someone's life, than someone's salvation, than revival in America?

As a well-known Disney character would say, "Let it go."

Chapter Ten

BARRIER

#10

DIVISION IN THE BODY

"My prayer is not for them [the disciples] alone. I also pray for those who will believe in me through their message, that all of them may be one . . ."

John 17:20–21

Now you are the body of Christ, and each one of you is a part of it.

I Corinthians 12: 27

Unity and harmony in the Church are important to Jesus, taking priority even over our acts of worship! In fact, from the Sermon on the Mount we can tell that conflict and strife stand in the way of worship. In other words, it is another barrier hindering our prayers.

> "Therefore, if you are offering your gift at the altar and there remember that your brother has something against you, leave your gift there in front of the altar. First go and be reconciled to your brother; then come and offer your gift."
>
> Matthew 5: 23, 24

Jesus was very clear not only about where He stands on interpersonal relationships, but also the importance of reconciliation, especially in the Body of Christ.

"He Started It!"

Sin rarely involves just one person, and the sin nature can come up with all kinds of reasons why our sin was someone else's fault. So many offenses are the result of an act of revenge for an earlier act of revenge, which was to avenge something else, which happened because . . . well, you get it. Just look at today's newspaper.

Perspective from *The Hunger Games*

Suzanne Collins' *Hunger Games* trilogy gives a chilling picture of the potential evil in the human heart. In Collins' description of a future America, the rich and pampered pit the children of the poor and powerless against one another in an arena created with deliberate cruelty. Here the young "tributes" fight to the death for the amusement of the safe and comfortable residents in "the Capital."

I read the first book a year ago and was hooked. I listened to the second and third books on audio while traveling, and so when the story got to what I considered the most important words in the series, I was hearing them.

As Katniss Everdeen, the young heroine, is heading for her second Hunger Games, her mentor gives her one final piece of advice:

"Remember who the real enemy is."

The line gave me a chill, not just because they stated the profound truth in the story, but because of their relevance to the Church. While the obvious enemy of the young gladiators in the story is the Capital, in real life the Church fails to recognize *our* real enemy. That enemy too often succeeds in pitting us against one another, dividing the Body of Christ, and making us ineffective, even as he persuades some of the Church that he (the enemy) doesn't even exist.

When a fellow human shows himself to be human, he doesn't need revenge and condemnation, he needs God's grace and compassion—and help.

Help him up!

As you may have experienced, those times of failure—when our impulse is to isolate ourselves—are times when we need one another more than ever. God never meant for the Christian faith to be "just me and Jesus." There are definitely times when dealing with sin is a team effort. James admonished the Church to "confess your sins to each other and pray for each other so that you may be healed . . ." (James 5:16) In this case, sin was interfering with healing! The rest of the verse says, "The prayer of a righteous man is *powerful and effective.*" [italics mine] "Righteous" does not refer to perfection, but to a forgiven believer, one with a clean slate. Don't we all want our prayers to be powerful and effective?

James closes his letter with this solemn reminder of our responsibility to the Church as a whole and our brothers and sisters individually:

> My brothers, if one of you should wander from the truth and someone should bring him back, remember this: Whoever turns a sinner from the error of his way will save him from death and cover over a multitude of sins.
>
> James 5:19–20

OK, but *how* does one "bring him back"? Jesus gave these practical guidelines for confronting a brother or sister regarding sin:

> "If your brother sins against you, go and show him his fault, just between the two of you. If he listens to you, you have won your brother over. But if he will not listen, take one or two others along, so that 'every matter may be established by the testimony of two or three witnesses.' If he refuses to listen to them, tell it to the church: and if he refuses to listen even to the church, treat him as you would a pagan or a tax collector."
>
> Matthew 18: 15–17

By this we see that the best way to approach an errant believer is as privately as possible. It may not be necessary to expose the person's sin to the whole church. In fact, undue humiliation may only serve to alienate the brother. On the other hand, if your first attempt at correction fails, taking one or two others along will prevent the "he said, she said" later that can cause a blowup and chaos in the church—just the sort of chaos Satan loves to see. Chaos is the opposite of what Jesus wants. As we saw in Chapter One, even in the last hours before His death, He was praying for His disciples, and for us, that we would be one in Him:

Submit—Seriously?

I Peter deals at length with order and relationships in society in general and within the Church in particular. The unpopular word "submit" appears more than some of us would like it to. I Peter 2:13–17 admonishes us to submit to the governing authorities. This, by the way, is the same Peter who had boldly said to the Sanhedrin "We must obey God rather than men!" (Acts 5:29) so there is a time when that choice must be made, and when a government commands us to do something contrary to God's commands, God's law must trump man's. But *in general* Christians should be known as respectful, peaceful, law-abiding citizens. Christian slaves are told to obey their masters, even the harsh ones, reminding us that Jesus suffered unjustly for us. Wives are told to submit to their husbands, even (especially?) unbelieving ones, describing true beauty as ". . . the unfading beauty of a gentle and quiet spirit, which is of great worth in God's sight." (I Peter 3: 4) Young men are told to respect the older ones in the Church. (I Peter 5:5)

However, Peter made it clear that the respect was to go both ways. "Finally, all of you, live in harmony with one another." (3: 8) "All of you, clothe yourselves with humility toward one another." (5:5b) Peter appealed to the elders as a fellow elder not to lord it over those under their authority but to be eager to *serve* (5:1–4)

Husbands are told, ". . . be considerate as you live with your wives and treat them with respect as the weaker partner and as heirs with you of the gracious gift of life . . ." (I Peter 3:7) Women who bristle at the word "weaker" should note that this is a word used to describe a delicate piece of fine china that has great value. Physical weakness does not constitute inequality in this verse, for Peter gives wives the radical title of "heirs with you" in a society where only sons received an inheritance.

A Special Note to Husbands

At the end of this husband/wife passage of I Peter is an interesting, not-so-subtle hint for husbands regarding unanswered prayer. After describing how wives should treat their husbands (with purity, reverence, and gentleness), verse 7 says:

> "Husbands, *in the same way* be considerate as you live with your wives, and treat them with respect as the weaker partner and as heirs with you of the gracious gift of life, *so that nothing will hinder your prayers.*" [italics mine]

If you are a married man who senses that your prayers are being hindered somehow, check your attitude toward your wife. Are you exercising your God-given authority over her with purity, reverence, and gentleness? Or are you treating her in ways that are not entirely Christ-like? Do you take her and what she does for you for granted? Have you failed to see her as a gift from God, a delicate treasure to be treated with gentleness and respect? (I know women can and should be strong, so this should not be done in a condescending way, but simple courtesy goes a long way.) This is the only scripture regarding relationships that I know of that mentions hindrance to prayer specifically, so I think it's worth noting.

In the interest of equal time, a word to wives, not from the apostle Peter, just from a sister who's one of you: Unfortunately, there are women who are not always receptive to courtesies men extend to them, and this may make men hesitant to try. (A woman comes to mind who grabbed a door handle away from a man who was holding the door open for her, saying, "Thank you, but we do these things for ourselves around here!") I have a bit of advice for you: as my daughter would say, "*Chill.*"

Here's a perspective for all of us: A man's holding a door open for a woman doesn't mean he thinks she's helpless. A woman's bringing a man a cup of coffee doesn't make her his slave. These are just the kind acts every Christian should be willing and in the habit of doing for one another as representatives of Christ, who after all gave His life for us. (We'd all be a lot happier, too.)

Maybe treating one another with consistent love and respect won't make every prayer get instantly answered, but it wouldn't hurt to try. I'm guessing the requests that don't get granted won't seem all that important after all. As we saw in Chapter Five, people and relationships are priority to God, and they should be to us as well.

Chapter Eleven

BARRIER

#11

VAGUENESS

Jesus stopped and called them. "What do you want me to do for you?" he asked.

Matthew 20:32

Could you be more specific, please?

In the above passage of Matthew, two blind men sitting by the roadside had heard that Jesus was passing by. They probably had heard of His healings and were understandably excited. They began shouting out, "Lord, Son of David, have mercy on us!" (vs. 30) The crowd tried to shut them up, but to their credit, they persevered, and Jesus stopped. He asked them, "What do you want me to do for you?"

Of course, it was obvious what they needed. Even if it wasn't that obvious, wouldn't Jesus have known? Was Jesus asking them for information, or was He wanting them to admit their need out loud?

I have in the past associated with believers whose approach to healing was to "claim it," that is, to speak what isn't as though it were. There is probably a time for that kind of faith, but I suspect that most of the time a Christian is only going to look foolish claiming to be "in divine health" when his outward appearance (red eyes, runny nose, cough, hoarseness, cast on the leg, etc.) clearly states otherwise.

Sometimes we should just admit we need Jesus' help, and it's OK that help sometimes takes time. (If you still want to practice "positive confession," you could say, "I'm *recovering* from a cold.") Sickness and other troubles, as we've discussed in other chapters, are this life's reminders of our constant dependence on God.

Shotgun or Laser?

A pastor I knew was challenging us to pray more specifically. He compared vague, general prayers to firing a shotgun and hoping we hit something. But, he said, a specific prayer is more like a well-aimed rifle; it will hit its target more often. "And a *very* specific prayer is like a laser . . . and a laser can cut through steel," he concluded. There is definitely a time to say "Thy will be done," and God does know best. But when Jesus taught His disciples the Lord's Prayer He didn't say "pray these words," He said "pray in this way." Sure, "Thy will be done . . ." but regarding *what?*

There is something about a specific answer to a specific prayer that not only builds our faith but makes us want to share it. I for one *love* to share stories about God's answers to my prayers . . . I guess you've figured that out by now.

Granted, God may say "yes," "no," or "wait." But if we never ask, we'll never know. And if we ask vague things like "God bless America!" how will we know when and how He's answered?

We may not know exactly how to pray, but God can help us. Again the key is to ask.

> "In the same way, the Spirit helps us in our weakness. We do not know what we ought to pray for, but the Spirit himself intercedes for us with groans that words cannot express. And he who searches our hearts knows the mind of the Spirit, because the Spirit intercedes for the saints in accordance with God's will."
>
> Romans 8: 26, 27

God knows exactly what we need, even when we don't. It has been my experience that when I don't know what to pray, He helps me, and sometimes even tells me *exactly what to pray!* The following story illustrates this experience. (This is a longer story than my usual anecdotes, but stay with me. It's a little embarrassing, and believe me, I wouldn't be sharing it if it weren't such a perfect example of a "laser beam prayer" and its result!)

Hand-picked by God

Our youngest daughter Kelly has had her problems in life, some of which I've related, but she loves Jesus, and I've been able to see His hand in her life, even when things seem to go awry.

In Port Huron a good number of high school graduates attend the community college before going out of town to a larger university. Since we have a good community college, this has always been a practical and economical choice, one which our son Ben made. Kelly, however, seemed anxious to spread her wings ASAP, and a girlfriend persuaded her that Grand Rapid Community College was better than the one close to home. We visited the school, and it did seem like a good school. However, this course of action had one little drawback: a community college does not have dormitories! Where would the girls live?

We made several trips to Grand Rapids to interview, apply, and attend orientations, and while there we of course looked for a place for the girls to stay. It was pretty clear that any money saved by attending a community college would be eaten up in rent, and after Kelly was enrolled, the situation was further complicated by her friend's informing her that they were moving to Louisiana, and she would not be going with Kelly to this school after all.

After the initial disappointment of that news, Kelly put out "feelers" to see if any of her other friends would be willing to share an apartment with her in the Grand Rapids area, and she reconnected with a friend from high school that I'll call "Jane". Jane had been a couple of years ahead of Kelly and was no longer in school, but she, too, was ready to get out of Port Huron and saw Kelly's proposal as an invitation to independence and adventures in faraway places, if you can call Grand Rapid "faraway."

Jane's finances were limited, and depending on what kind of employment she could find in another part of the state, might remain limited, so low rent was a "must." We visited various low-budget areas of Grand Rapids, Holland, and Wyoming (the town, not the state—we're not *that* adventurous.). While the places we looked at weren't exactly my cup of tea, Kelly seemed almost intoxicated with the prospect of being independent. While I cringed at the cracks and peeling paint and kept in mind that the building inspector wouldn't be allowing these places on the market if they were hazardous, Kelly was excited about anything that had running water and a kitchen.

We finally settled on one of four apartments in a building on the corner of two main roads. Although the apartment had definitely seen better days, it seemed quiet and was situated on a relatively pleasant street lined with trees and near a wooded area. We signed the paperwork while the property manager chatted with us and recommended a church nearby for the girls to check out.

When it was time to move, Jane was not available to join us quite yet, but we had enough to do without her. Kelly and I packed her car to the gills and headed over on a Friday afternoon. After unloading what we had and taking a closer look at just what Kelly had got herself into, we headed for Walmart and loaded the car with cleaning supplies, after which we worked until midnight getting rid of as many spots, smudges, sticky things, and nasty smells as we could. This involved wiping virtually every surface in the place, including the insides of drawers and the refrigerator. (You would have to know how much I hate cleaning to know what a labor of love this was.) There were some mishaps, like blinds that fell apart as we tried to wipe them off (Oh well, privacy is overrated anyway.) and windows that wouldn't open. This was a problem, as it was July, and the place had no air conditioning. In the wee hours of the morning Kelly discovered that one of her "quiet" neighbors liked to play his boom box at top volume in the middle of the night. I remember thinking, "Well, she's here for an education. She's going to find out how the other half lives."

Early the next morning I took a walk, timing how long it took to get to the bus stop where Kelly would be catching her rides to class, then in the other direction, enjoying the cool green of the woods and trying to ignore the trash left by inconsiderate passers-through. I then helped Kelly put away the rest of what we had brought the night before to get ready for the next wave of stuff.

About midmorning Marty came, followed by Kelly's boyfriend,

Jordan, and along with them two more carloads of furniture and other supplies. As we were bringing things in, one of Kelly's new neighbors walked right in and said "hello." I was a little surprised at his lack of inhibition, but in talking with him soon realized he was somewhat mentally challenged. Again, I thought this would be a good opportunity for Kelly to practice tolerance and learn about people with special needs. When the young man's girlfriend showed up and started to tell me about the voices she always heard telling her to kill herself, I thought, *OK, Lord, do we really need this much opportunity?!* Since she claimed to be a Christian, I talked with her, shared some scriptures with her about spiritual warfare, and prayed with her, while her boyfriend continued to wander about the place commenting on the bad shape everything was in.

We then met Kelly's neighbors across the hall, a mother with her daughter who appeared to be about thirteen. I introduced myself and Kelly, and apologized for making so much noise vacuuming the night before. "I hope I didn't disturb you."

"Oh, *you* didn't disturb me," she replied, glaring at the self-designated building inspector, who happened to be the one whose boom box had been blaring in the wee hours of the morning. She then hurried her daughter out. Ordinarily I might have thought they had someplace urgent to go, but a moment before I had seen something in the woman's eyes that caused me some concern: fear.

The concern only grew when we saw the "laundry room," a tiny cubicle with one washer, one dryer, and one door. It looked like the perfect place to be cornered and assaulted.

"Kelly, I want you to *always* take your laundry to the laundromat, understand?"

"O . . . K . . ." I could see Kelly was beginning to be uneasy, too.

Jordan confirmed our uneasiness when he said, "Kelly, I don't feel right about this area. It reminds me of where I grew up, and that was *not* a good neighborhood." I was impressed that he would offer this opinion before either Marty or I had said a word. I was also starting to get a sick feeling in my stomach. Maybe we had finally gone too far in letting Kelly have her way.

As I sat in Kelly's bedroom, praying, there was conversation in the living room, and when I came out, everyone looked serious; Kelly was white with fear.

"Mom, tell me what to do." *Wow, I haven't heard that in a while.*

The final nail in the coffin of this venture was a scene that Marty and Jordan had witnessed outside. A car much too expensive for that neighborhood pulled quickly into the driveway next door, and a man jumped out and went inside with something in his hand. Moments later he came back out, now empty-handed, hopped back in, and screeched away.

Just as the men were wondering if that was what it had appeared to be, they saw a repeat of the scenario with a different car, different guy.

"Kelly, you're not staying here." That was it. Never mind that the papers have been signed for a year's worth of rent, no amount of savings, education, or independence was worth putting our daughter at risk. Kelly had no argument.

"What do I do, Mom?"

"You're asking my opinion?" (Hey, I just wanted to make sure before meddling!)

"Well," I began, "Whatever you do, you need to *bathe it in prayer.*" But as I gave her this advice I began questioning how much—or how little—*I* had prayed about this venture. *Shame on me!* "Let's ask God to show us what He wants us to do."

Kelly agreed readily, and we immediately prayed, asking for direction. For some reason we took out Kelly's schedule and perhaps for the first time looked at the location of her classes. Not all of them were in Grand Rapids. In fact, every class but one was in Holland! And here she was in Wyoming, with a bus that went to Grand Rapids but none to Holland.

Needless to say, we felt more than a little foolish.

Immediately Kelly and Jordan got out their laptops to start searching for apartments in Holland. By this time we just wanted something safe, even if it was out of Jane's price range. When Kelly wondered what she was going to tell Jane, the obvious answer was to tell her the truth. After all, Jane wouldn't want to live in that kind of place, either. Marty said that if we couldn't get the girls out of the contract, he was willing to pay the rent for as long as it took.

We learned at that moment that this apartment didn't even have internet access, and Jordan mentioned seeing a coffeehouse down the road that had it, so we grabbed our laptops and headed out for coffee.

As Kelly, Jordan and I got our coffees and sat down to look for apartments, we didn't notice at first that Marty was lagging behind. When he came in a few minutes later, he sat next to me and said, "Well, I think you have your answer." I was curious. Then as he related what had just happened, I was awestruck.

As we had come into the coffeehouse, a man had been standing between the two doors in the entryway. Although I don't remember seeing him, Marty had, and although Marty is not a very social person and practically never strikes up a conversation with a stranger, today was an exception. I got goose bumps as I heard him tell the story:

"Excuse me, do you live around here?" Marty asked.

"Yes, I've lived here all my life," the man replied.

"Would you say Wyoming is a safe town to live in?"

"Oh yes, it's a great little town. I've been a real estate agent here for twenty years, so I know it very well. And for the most part it's very nice."

"That's good to hear, because we're thinking of getting our daughter an apartment here." (Marty didn't tell him we already had signed the lease, and that she was already moved in.)

"Really? Whereabouts?"

"On ________ Street." [*Tense pause*]

"*Where* on __________ Street?" the man asked, suddenly sounding concerned.

Marty named the two streets that intersected.

"You do *not* want her there," the man stated without hesitation. Marty must have looked startled to have received such blunt advice from a virtual stranger, so the real estate agent explained. "There are two buildings on that corner with four apartments each, and they're where all the drug deals take place."

At that moment Marty confessed that we had already moved Kelly into one of those eight apartments.

"Get her out of there, *NOW*." The man ordered with authority.

As Marty told the story, I couldn't help thinking of the angels that came to Lot and ordered him to take his family out of Sodom and Gomorrah before it perished in fire and brimstone, and I seriously wondered whether this man had been a real estate agent or an angel. (He was gone by the time Marty finished telling us about the conversation.) Whether man or angel, he obviously knew what he was talking about, and we were quite willing to take his word for it.

It had taken us about 24 hours to get Kelly moved into the apartment; it took less than an hour and a half to get her out. We crammed everything into the three cars and left in a cloud of dust without looking back. As we pulled out, I tried not to think about all the hours we had put into cleaning every corner of every room. (*I wish I'd spent all that time and energy cleaning my house!)*

Now all that remained was to deal with the lease agreement. Monday morning we called the property manager and put the phone on "speaker."

"Let me do the talking," Marty said, and I thought, *No problem!* I was feeling pretty naïve and was glad to have an assertive man willing to deal with our predicament.

Marty told the manager very frankly about his concerns, and when he described what he had seen, the young woman sounded stunned. (Could she have been as naïve as we had?) She didn't argue with him about our concerns, but said she would put the apartment back up for rent. We would be responsible to pay the rent until someone else wanted it. (I silently prayed that she was truly putting it back on the market and that she wouldn't take advantage of our situation.)

Wanting to stay on the right track, I said, "OK, now we just have to pray that someone else rents it . . ."

But then it occurred to me—*Wait a minute . . . WHO?* I certainly wouldn't want *someone else's* daughters renting it! Or young newlyweds. *Or* a family with young children. *Or* a family with teenagers. *Or* an elderly couple . . .

Lord, I prayed, *I don't want Marty to have to pay thousands of dollars for my stupidity.* (I still blamed myself for not having seen that it was not a good place for Kelly.)

I then had another thought—for the woman with the young daughter, the young man who was mentally challenged, his girlfriend who heard voices. God loved them, too!

Lord, who do <u>*You*</u> *want living there? Help me to pray Your will.*

Moments later I believe God showed me His will in detail, and I knew exactly how to pray.

And Lord, I added at the end of the prayer, *if You bring that person to rent the apartment, I promise I won't complain about all the time spent cleaning or consider it wasted time, but I'll offer it as a sacrifice—a labor of love for You.*

Two weeks later we got a phone call from the property manager, saying they had found a renter for the apartment.

"I've never had a property move so quickly!" she exclaimed. I was glad to hear it, but still concerned for the safety of whoever was going to be in that apartment, in that environment.

"Can you tell me about the renter?" I asked. The manager hesitated, and I thought perhaps I might have asked her to break some kind of property managers' rule. So I asked, "How about if I tell you what kind of person I was praying for, and you tell me if that's who rented the apartment?"

". . . OK . . ." I couldn't tell if she was intrigued or just thought I was a little strange.

"I prayed for a young, single man, Christian, street-smart, strong both physically and spiritually, who understands spiritual warfare. . . . How'd I do?"

After a pause, she said, "Well, he *is* a young, single man, and his pastor came with him to sign the papers. He's been out of prison for ten years, and believe it or not, this apartment is a step *up* for him."

WOW, I thought. *I hadn't thought to pray for an ex-convict! Nice touch!* The fact that the man had been in prison assured me that he was not as naïve as . . . some of us. On the other hand, the fact that he had been able to stay out of trouble for ten years said something about his character, and the fact that his pastor was there with him assured me that he had a good Christian support system, probably some accountability, too.

But in case I had any doubts, the last thing the property manager said was the icing on the cake: "Oh, and he's *thrilled* with the apartment. He said "I can't believe how *clean* it is!"

YESSSSSSS!!!! Thank you, Lord! I prayed as I felt my sacrifice being accepted.

Before hanging up I got the man's first name so Kelly and I could pray for him. I don't know what ever happened with him, but I expect someday I might hear the story from the man himself, when we have all eternity to testify to one another about Gods specific answers to specific prayers. My stories will probably include another example that began in 1994...

Too Important To Be Vague About

"Mom, I don't think I'm ever gonna get married," my oldest daughter Joanna lamented one day. "I'm the only one in my class that's not dating anybody."

Now ordinarily when my children are hurting I take it very seriously, but I must admit my first impulse that day was to disagree with her assessment of the situation.

"Oh I don't know about that, honey. For one thing, you're fifteen years old," I pointed out. Joanna wasn't exactly over the hill yet. "And secondly, look around. Do you see anybody you want to spend the rest of your life with?"

"NO!" she cried, looking slightly nauseated at the thought.

"Tell you what," I suggested. "How about making a list of the top ten things you're looking for in a mate—that's 'mate', *not 'date'*. (Never mind the nice hair and a cool car.)" She got the idea.

A short time later, she showed me her list, and I must say I was impressed. At the very top, Number One Qualification was "100% sold out to God." *OK, we're off to a good start . . .*

Number Two: "Zany sense of humor like mine." *Of course, you gotta have fun . . .* The list included things like "loves children," "shares my taste in music," and (one that would definitely narrow down the list of candidates) "virgin." I was pretty proud of my daughter's standards. The closest thing on the list to "good-looking" was that she wanted someone who was active and in good shape. In other words, she didn't want to be married to a couch potato. I commended her for her vision. Then I said, "OK, now let's pray."

We took the list and prayed over it, that wherever this guy was—if there were such a guy—that God would keep him, and that at the right time He would bring him and Joanna together.

And she waited.

Two years later Joanna graduated from high school, not having met Mr. Right. She went on to college and discovered that one of her girlfriends also had a list, and they compared notes, and kept praying for each other and for their future mates. And Joanna kept waiting.

At one point I got a letter from Joanna saying she was beginning to doubt that such a man existed. Even just the first two items on her list rarely, if ever, seemed to show up in the same person. "There are some really funny guys here, but they don't take God seriously. And the ones that take God seriously take *everything else* seriously, and they're no fun to be with!" Marty and I sensed her frustration and tried to encourage her that sometimes the best takes time, but it's also worth waiting for.

The summer of her sophomore year Joanna volunteered at a Christian camp in another part of the state. When she came to our family summer home for a weekend visit, she brought three friends with her, one of whom was a young man named Sean, who just happened to be from Port Huron! In fact, he had been living ten minutes from us most of his life but had never met Joanna before camp, because he had attended a different school and his family belonged to a different church.

By now you've probably figured out how this story ends. The "sold-out-to-God" qualification was evident, not just because Sean was volunteering at a Christian camp, but also because his ambition was to be a chaplain in the Army. (And the military takes care of the "couch potato" concern.) He had the sense of humor Joanna loved, and whether he was leading youth at church or working at the camp, Sean was frequently seen with laughing children hanging from every limb. In fact, I think it's fair to say he fulfilled every request Joanna had made that day as a lonely fifteen-year-old.

I guess I should say *God* fulfilled every request of that detailed prayer our daughter had prayed repeatedly over the years.

In preparation for the Army Sean attended the Citadel, and one weekend when Joanna came out to see him, he proposed to her in a restaurant in Charlotte, North Carolina . . . which may or may not explain why their first two children are named Caroline and Charlotte. Those little girls and their baby brother, Jackson Henry, are further proof that this is literally a match made in heaven. Not perfect by any means, because Joanna and Sean are imperfect people like the rest of us. As with any marriage, they haven't exactly "lived happily ever after." Their "ever after" has included two lonely years of separation due to Sean's deployments—one year in Iraq, one year in Afghanistan. And of course parenthood carries with it its own set of trials and struggles and sleepless nights.

No, "happily ever after" isn't nearly as interesting as real life, with its challenges—a.k.a., opportunities to exercise faith. (How else are we going to experience the thrill of seeing God give us specific answers to our prayers?)

Just Because

Just before Easter I was reading a devotional about prayer that had the same scripture I opened this chapter with, and as I prayed that morning, I heard Still Small Voice ask, *What do you want Me to do for you?* I continued my daily prayers, trying to be more specific. I prayed at length for my family members (by name, by need) and my neighbors, friends, and country. Apparently I wasn't finished, because Still Small Voice said again, *What do you want Me to do for **you**?*

I thought, *for me? I don't need anything.* I was pretty content. Then I realized He had said, "*What do you **want** Me to do for you?*" I felt a flutter of excitement. Was Jesus offering to do something for me "just because"—just to make me happy because I was His child? I thought of "The Power of the Cross," the gorgeous song I had just recently learned, which had become my new favorite. I could play it on the guitar, but it sounded especially beautiful on the harp, and at that time of year the words were especially appropriate.

"I want to sing 'The Power of the Cross' at the Maundy Thursday service!" I blurted.

I felt a little silly. Maundy Thursday was three days away and was no doubt already planned out. In the twenty-two years we had attended that church I had never *gone* to the Maundy Thursday service before, much less participated, so I wasn't even sure what was involved. Besides, this was a church that was loaded with talent, and it had been over a decade since I'd been asked to sing a solo. Pastor Bruce, the music director, had heard me sing at funerals and weddings, and he had never taken me up on my offer to sing any time he wanted. I wasn't about to offer again and create an awkward situation, so I left it with Jesus and went on with my day.

I did sing the song and one other for the ladies at my Bible study the next day. A song or two from me had become part of our weekly meetings, and they were especially taken with the two I sang that day. One of them said, "You need to tell Pastor Bruce about those songs so the choir can sing them!" I thought it was a good idea, so I made a mental note to tell him next time I saw him.

I didn't have to wait long. When the Bible study was over, as I was walking out the door, Pastor Bruce was just walking by.

"Pastor Bruce! I'm supposed to tell you about two songs!" I said.

"Which two?" he asked, never slowing his pace. I called out the names of the two songs as he thanked me, rounded the corner and disappeared.

Oh well, I've told him, I thought. Again, I didn't give it another thought.

Later that day the phone rang. It was Pastor Bruce.

"What were those two songs you were telling me about?" he asked. I told him the name of the first one. Moments later I could hear it playing in the background and realized he was on his computer looking up the songs.

The other one is "The Power of the Cross," I said, and as he heard it, he exclaimed, "Oh! We've done that one for an Easter musical. Good song!"

"Yeah, I love it," I said. "It works well with my harp."

After a pause he said, "Um . . . what are you doing Thursday night?"

It occurred to me that Thursday night was the Maundy Thursday service, so I said with a grin Pastor Bruce couldn't see, "Umm . . . what *am* I doing Thursday night?"

You can probably guess the rest.

I've gone to great lengths to persuade my readers that God's will for us isn't just to make us healthy, wealthy, and happy. But that doesn't mean He will never do something for us just to remind us, "Hey, I love you!" As I have often explained to my children, that's the message in a beautiful sunrise, a flower that seemingly exists just to give pleasure . . .

Or a specific answer to a specific request for something non-crucial, "just because."

However, there also may be a time when you feel led to pray for something specific that is way more important than wanting to sing a song for a service. If prayer is the most powerful force in the world, God could be calling you commit to pray in a specific area, daily, indefinitely. This was my experience in the summer of 2005, and what He led me to pray has been part of my daily prayers ever since. (If this story sounds familiar, it may be because I incorporated it at the end of Sparrows, the third book in my *Awakening* trilogy.)

A New Approach to the War on Terror

It was a beautiful day in July, 2005. I was sitting in the sunshine on the beach of Lake Michigan, thinking about terrorism . . . OK, I'm a little weird . . . but something I had heard on the news was tugging at my heart. Recently the subway system in London had been bombed. People were killed, and others injured. Flashbacks of 9/11 came, and I began praying for the victims and their families. Something was bothering me—frustrating me. Why was I always praying about these things *after* the fact? Wasn't there some way I could pray that these things wouldn't happen in the first place?

I thought about the pastor who had talked about the most effective prayers being *specific*—not vague, "shotgun" prayers. I wanted my prayer to be that well-aimed rifle, even a spiritual laser. After all, these were human lives at risk!

But how do we get specific when we don't know who the enemy is, where they are, what they have planned, and who their target is? I asked the Lord how I could narrow the subject down, and I think He answered, because the thought immediately dropped into my mind: *Pray against what they have planned for today.*

So I prayed for anyone who planned to be a suicide bomber *that day*, that God would change their minds, maybe even their hearts, so they would renounce their hatred and embrace His mercy. Knowing that God doesn't violate anyone's free will, I also prayed about those whose hearts were hardened and whose minds were set on murder. I prayed that *that day* their communications would fail (their computers would crash, their cell phones disconnect) their transportation would break down, their calculations be wrong, their timing be off, their weapons malfunction, and their bombs fail to detonate. I prayed that the enemy's camp would be thrown into confusion, and that even then some of them might repent and be saved. I prayed for whoever were the targets of terrorism *that day*, especially the ones who weren't yet ready to meet God face to face, not only that He would save their lives, but that they would *know* He had done it and devote the rest of their lives to finding, serving, and honoring Him.

I prayed for every branch of our military by name, for our intelligence, security, and law enforcement, that God would give them discernment, boldness, and protection as they confronted evil *that day*. I also prayed for their (legitimate) counterparts in other parts of the world.

There turned out to be a lot of specific things to pray, once I narrowed it down to that one day. Of course, that meant I was to pray again the next day, and the next.

The next day I heard the news—Four more bombs were discovered in the London subways. This time three of them had been duds, and the fourth detonated only partially and hadn't hurt anyone. It then occurred to me that prayer is our weapon to fight terrorism. After all, who but God knows the identity, location, and plans of every terrorist on the planet? Only He has the power to hold back the tide of violence.

I have been praying variations of that original prayer daily since 2005. I can't help wondering how many of us God has praying in this way, because I have a growing folder full of answers to these prayers. It contains news clippings about foiled terrorist attacks and stories from ministries about suicide bombers who had a vision of Jesus and changed their minds. Some of these former would-be terrorists are now evangelizing and planting churches in their part of the world!

Lately, however, things are beginning to heat up, and terrorism world-wide has become a greater threat than ever. It is time to enlist more prayer support. There are some who question how much longer God's hand of mercy and protection will remain with this nation if we as a people do not repent and get back to Him. Repentance and revival in America should certainly be among the daily requests of the "remnant" who are still trying to stay faithful to the LORD. In the meantime, as James 5:16 in the King James Version says, "The effectual, fervent prayer of a righteous man availeth much." Or as the Message puts it, "The prayer of a person living right with God is something powerful to be reckoned with."

Do you believe that? Do you *really* believe it? Are you willing to stand in the gap daily for whatever God is leading you to pray about? Your calling may be regarding terrorism. If so, an example of what I pray daily can be found in the back of this book.

Your calling may be something different. For example, at a ladies' prayer conference Beth Coppedge had a globe and a world map in front of the sanctuary, and we were encouraged to pick a nation to pray for daily. With my deployed son-in-law in mind, I thought Kelly and I would pray for Afghanistan, but Kelly wanted to spin the globe and "let God decided." Her finger landed on Libya, and I've prayed daily for that nation ever since.

I know a woman who prays daily for the unborn in much the same way I pray for victims of terrorism. I am not writing this to tell you *what* to pray about, but to say that God could very well lead you into something very specific, and to encourage you to be obedient if you hear such a call.

A Spiritual Ephod

At a major prayer gathering in Detroit, the crowd was encouraged to take seriously their role as priests, who in Old Testament times represented the people before the LORD. Each priest wore a rectangular piece of cloth called an "ephod" over his hearts whenever he approached the Lord's presence. Sewn into each ephod were twelve precious stones, representing the twelve tribes of Israel, and one of the jobs of the priests was to bring these twelve tribes before the LORD in prayer.

The participants in the prayer meeting were encouraged to make a list of twelve unsaved people they knew, for whom they could pray daily. As the twelve precious stones were in four rows of three, the names we chose were in four categories. That day several thousand Christians were each encouraged to pray daily for three unsaved family members, three unsaved neighbors, three unsaved friends, and three unsaved (as far as we know) strangers, or people who do not know us by name, such as a celebrity, political leader, or relative of a friend. As the thousands of attendees scribbled names into notebooks and onto scraps of paper, the speaker encouraged us to imagine the number of unsaved people being prayed for specifically, by name, every day. Think of the possibilities of such a flood of prayer!

If you have slipped into the attitude of seeing prayer as a chore or a bore, it may be time to pray more specifically. Then watch for the specific answers, and get ready to be excited again.

Chapter Twelve

BARRIER #12

INGRATITUDE

"When I fed them, they were satisfied; when they were satisfied, they became proud; then they forgot me."

Hosea 13: 6

The Trouble with Blessings

As I hope I have made clear, God *wants* to bless His people! But anyone who has observed a child who has been given an abundance of gifts could tell you that human nature does not always lean toward perpetual thankfulness. When blessings are abundant, gratitude is spontaneous at the beginning, then short-lived, and virtually non-existent sooner or later (more often sooner than later).

The truth is, most of us have been given far more blessings than we thank God for, and way more than we can even count. If you doubt this, consider God's first and greatest gift to you—He created you! And if you're reading this book, it means He has given you miraculous organs called "eyes," which are so complex it takes years in medical school just to begin to understand how they work. And think of what your eyes can see—shapes, textures, shadows, and an almost infinite number of colors, not to mention the precious faces of people you love.

Of course, God's creating you would be meaningless if you lived on earth for a few short years, only to die and spend eternity lost and apart from Him. But God so loved *you* that He gave His only begotten Son to pay the price for your sins, blunders, faults, mistakes, and imperfections, to make you, His bride, pure and blameless.

If that were the only thing God ever did for us, it would be worth thanking Him forever just for the fact that we don't have to spend eternity in hell. But if that isn't mind-boggling enough, add to it the fact that Jesus has gone to prepare a place for us, His Bride, and that we get to spend the rest of eternity with the One who loves us, in indescribably happiness and peace. We could thank Him every minute of every day and not thank Him enough for that kind of love.

How to be Happy

We lived in Michigan for thirty years, but for some years our children have all been in either Kentucky or Tennessee. So I have spent a lot of time on the road, especially with the advent of grandchildren. One day I was heading out from Louisville to drive home by myself, and I recognized an opportunity to get in a good quantity of prayer time, which I was hoping would also be *quality* prayer time.

I decided that for the first portion of the trip I wouldn't ask God for anything, but I would just praise Him for everything He had given me. (Well, as much as I could think of, anyway. I will probably never be able to thank Him for *everything*.)

I began by thanking Him for creating me, and that all of my five senses worked. I thanked Him for things that blessed me through those senses: flowers, sunsets, smiles, and other things that blessed my eyes; for the sounds of every genre of music I enjoy—which is just about all of them; for foods that blessed my taste buds with a huge variety of flavors (I spent about five minutes just giving thanks for specific fruits and vegetables!); for aromas and fragrances that lifted my mood or reminded me of good times past; and for the good feelings of cool breezes, hot baths, and loving arms.

Besides seeing, hearing, tasting, smelling, and feeling, I thanked Him for all the other things I could do—walk, talk, sing, play instruments, hug children, tell stories, read good books, learn new things, drive a car, ride a bike, and paddle a kayak.

I thanked the Lord for everything about my family that I loved, especially things that I knew were missing in many families—healthy children, intact marriages, good times with my parents when I was growing up, reunions, weddings, holidays, and just "hanging out." I thanked Him for creating humor and that laughter is a pleasure that's actually good for us.

I thanked the Lord for all the privileges of living in a country which (so far) gives us the freedom to worship Him whenever, wherever, and however we want. I thanked Him for my church and for gifted writers, singers, and songwriters that glorify Him with their talents. I went on to thank Him for dozens of my favorite songs and books by name.

I thanked God for the flood of good memories that were bombarding my mind, until I was overwhelmed with how blessed I have been.

When I had thanked God for the positive blessings for a long time, I started to list a string of bad things. I thanked Him for protecting me from the horrible things that had never happened to me, for delivering me from the things that had, and most of all for all the torture He endured out of love for me.

I thanked Him all the way to Cincinnati. That's about 90 minutes. I only stopped because I needed to fill my tank, and I'm sure the people at the gas station wondered about the lady with the silly grin on her face. I could feel my heart bubbling over with joy.

So I thanked Him that thanks begets thanks.

God's Pet Peeve

> Now the people complained about their hardships in the hearing of the LORD, and when he heard them his anger was aroused.
>
> Numbers 11: 1

Just as gratitude is contagious, an ungrateful attitude can also spread like gangrene. Imagine being one of the children of Israel wandering in the desert. Someone complains about being unsure where you'll be traveling today. Someone else is griping about the manna that has been breakfast, lunch, and dinner for the past month, and yet another is wistfully thinking of the great foods that used to be served in Egypt. Never mind that your memories of the meals you had while in slavery don't exactly fit his description. The comments were made, and now you're finding you have a bad attitude and are contributing some complaints of your own.

But suppose one person begins recalling how awesome it was to see God's hand in the way the Red Sea opened up to let you all pass through. Suppose another started humming the song that Miriam and the women sang at the banks of the sea on the other side after your enemies were drowned and you realized you were free at last. Suppose someone shared how seeing the pillar of cloud by day and the fire by night brought them comfort, because it meant God was still with you. With two different attitudes going, which camp would you have been in?

We have no evidence that anyone besides a handful of men—Moses, Aaron, Hur, Joshua, and Caleb—kept a good outlook during these times. And not even all of these men were consistently grateful and faithful. And the Bible says God was very angry with the others, sometimes angry enough to want to destroy them.

Self-talk

The Bible was advocating good self-talk long before modern psychology ever came up with the term. "Praise the Lord, O my soul;" wrote the psalmist, "all my inmost being praise his holy name." (Psalm 103:1) Hearing yourself speaking (or singing) about God's goodness will reinforce thankfulness and be a blessing not only to God but to you. Conversely, if you hear yourself complaining all the time . . .

Psalm 50:14 says "Sacrifice thank offerings to God." It's true that there will be times when you won't *feel* like thanking God, but that doesn't mean that you can't do it anyway. (There it is again– that feeling vs. obeying issue.) When everything in your flesh is protesting but you thank Him anyway, consider it a sacrifice, given willfully to honor God.

I Thessalonians 5: 18 says to ". . . give thanks in all circumstances, for this is God's will for you in Christ Jesus." It says nothing about feeling like it, but you may feel like it later if you obey now.

Corrie Ten Boom's book *The Hiding Place* tells the story of how Corrie and her sister Betsie went through unspeakable suffering in a Nazi concentration camp. At one point, in spite of their circumstances, they decided to spend some time thanking God. At first it was for things that were obvious blessings—that they were together (Many families were split up.) and that the Lord had helped them get a Bible past the guard so that they could read and teach it while they were there. But when Betsie thanked God for the fleas in their barracks, Corrie refused to thank Him for that. Betsie didn't know *why* she was thanking Him for the fleas, except that they were part of the place He had sent them to, but she and Corrie were both to find out later what a blessing these little creatures were.

One night a fight broke out in the barracks, and someone called for a guard to come intervene. The guard refused to come in—because of the fleas. It was then that Corrie and Betsie realized why the guards had never come in to break up their nightly Bible studies. While they were sharing God's gift of life with the other women there, the fleas had been standing guard.

Thanking the LORD when we don't feel like it can open a window to some of the secrets of God's plan that we would never see otherwise. Do you want to have a more intimate relationship with God? Do you want Him to share His secrets with you?

Let's start thanking Him, whether we feel like it or not.

Chapter Thirteen

BARRIER #13

SPIRITUAL WARFARE

Then [the angel] continued, "Do not be afraid, Daniel. Since the first day that you set your mind to gain understanding and to humble yourself before your God, your words were heard, and I have come in response to them. But the prince of the Persian kingdom resisted me twenty-one days. Then Michael, one of the chief princes, came to help me, because I was detained there with the king of Persia."

Daniel 10: 12, 13

Finally, be strong in the Lord and in his mighty power. Put on the full armor of God so that you can take your stand against the devil's schemes. For our struggle is not against flesh and blood, but against the rulers, against the authorities, against the powers of this dark world and against the spiritual forces of evil in the heavenly realms.

Ephesians 6:10–12

I don't know of anyone who hasn't experienced the frustration of having their prayers go unanswered—or seemingly unanswered. I was pretty much at the end of my rope the night I watched my daughter suffer yet another excruciating migraine, with no apparent results from 12 years of prayers for her. Adding to the frustration was the fact that a couple of nights before, I had witnessed a miraculous healing of a cat I had struck with my minivan going 40 mph. (If this scenario doesn't ring a bell, go back and read the prologue, and don't ever skip the prologue again!)

I declared through angry tears that someday I would meet God face to face, and He would explain to me why one prayer for a stupid cat resulted in a virtual resurrection, while twelve years of prayers for my precious daughter seemed futile. While this was an angry prayer, this was not a prayer of unbelief, by the way. I really did believe (1) that the Lord was listening, (2) that He was in control, (3) that He had His reasons for everything, and (4) that *someday* He would explain it all to me. The last thing I expected was an answer that very night. But there have been times when God has surprised me, and this was one of them. The Still, Small Voice spoke to my heart, saying, *You don't have to wait that long. I'll explain it now.*

Part of me thought what my spirit had "heard" was just some wishful thinking out of my overactive imagination, but I stilled my heart the best I could to see if Still, Small Voice would say any more.

I truly believe it was God speaking to me, because (1) it made sense, (2) I'm pretty sure I couldn't have come up with this kind of answer on my own, and (3) it was much more concise and to-the-point than anything I would have said.

There's a battle going on for Kelly. But Satan didn't care about the cat.

I stood there for a moment, letting the thought sink in. It made sense.

Of course! Kelly is much more valuable than a cat. She is a child of God, born again, bright, gifted, and with her whole life ahead of her. She loves the Lord with all her heart and is ready to go anywhere, do anything for Him. Why *wouldn't* Satan paint a target on her?

I've often heard it said, "If it's important to you, it's important to God." But I had never taken it a step further and realized that if it's important to me and it's important to God, the enemy is going to fight me on it.

While on the one hand, it was disturbing to think that Satan was sending his minions to torment my daughter, on the other hand to think that the devil saw my daughter as a threat, even as a four-year-old . . . well, as the kids say, "That's pretty awesome!"

So what could I do that night but to dig in my heels and determine that I was in this battle, too, and that I wasn't going to quit fighting for my child? After all, God made her for a purpose, and He is bigger than migraines, bigger than discouragement, bigger than anything else the enemy might throw at us. "If God is for us, who can be against us?" (Romans 8:31)

You're in the Army now.

There's more to "fighting the good fight" than digging in our heels and putting up our fists. Fortunately the Bible has much to say about this unseen war that is being waged and how we are to win it.

If fighting in a war is something you'd just as soon "pass" on, you may be disappointed to learn that as a Christian you have no choice. When we give ourselves to Christ, we become soldiers in the biggest, most important battle of all time. The only alternative is not to commit to Christ, but if that's the case, you are already one of the enemy's prisoners.

You may be familiar with Paul's admonition to the Ephesians to "put on the whole armor of God." As this passage indicates, these are instructions on how to prepare to battle the enemy and still be standing when it's all over.

> Therefore put on the whole armor of God, so that when the day of evil comes, you may be able to stand your ground, and after you have done everything, to stand. Stand firm then, with the belt of truth buckled around your waist, and with the breastplate of righteousness in place, and with your feet fitted with the readiness that comes from the gospel of peace. In addition to all this, take up the shield of faith, with which you can extinguish all the flaming arrows of the evil one. Take the helmet of salvation and the sword of the Spirit, which is the word of God.
>
> Ephesians 6: 13–17

The Belt of Truth

Stand firm, then, with the belt of truth buckled around your waist . . .

Ephesians 6: 14

For a first century soldier, the belt had at least two purposes. If the soldier wore a loose-fitting garment, the belt held it in place so that he wouldn't get entangled and tripped up in the battle. The belt also held his weapon.

For a soldier of God the Truth is central to our warfare. Knowing the truth keeps us from getting entangled in the world's affairs, and this truth is expressed in the Word of God—the Bible—which is our "sword of the Spirit."

Today belts have other purposes, and although the image of a warrior's belt holding the sword of the Spirit is the most fitting, for a visual person like me, thinking about other kinds of belts helps drive home the importance of knowing (and practicing) the truth.

I recently heard a Bible teacher talk about the tool belts many workers use every day. Having every tool within reach helps them to get the job done more quickly and efficiently. Similarly, the more we know God's Word, the more thoroughly we can accomplish the work He has given us to do without being confused or slowed down by Satan's mixed messages.

There are the belts we buckle whenever we get into a car, which keep us safe in a collision. When unexpected calamity strikes our lives, as happens to us all at one time or another (or many times), knowing the truth (example: "Never will I leave you; never will I forsake you." Hebrews 13:5) keeps us from permanently injuring our faith.

If you have ever been water skiing, you might have worn a "ski belt," so that when you let go of the line you won't sink and drown. Similarly, knowing the truth ("I can do everything through him who gives me strength."—Philippians 4:13) can help you "keep your head above water" rather than being overwhelmed by the tasks you face.

I was sitting in my lounge chair one morning, "putting on the belt of truth," and an image popped into my mind of God's arms around my waist, buckling the belt for me, while at the same time enfolding me in His love. It was a warm, secure feeling, one that made me picture my daughter Joanna with one of her little ones held in a sling, close to her heart. I know that's not exactly a belt, but knowing the truth does help me feel secure and close to God.

The most recent image of a belt that came to me during my devotional time is the one that excites me the most. It occurred to me that mountain climbers wear special belts, too—belts that keep them from falling and that connect them to someone else higher up. It is this belt that enables them to scale the heights, knowing that if they slip they won't go tumbling all the way back down the mountain and have to start all over, assuming they survive! With the belt that connects them to the person above them, they can get up where they are, regain their grip, and continue from where they slipped.

Only God knows what heights He is taking us to, as the truth is revealed to us, but if and when we fail, our failure doesn't mean we have to "backslide" and start all over at Square One. We need only confess, repent, and press on. (I John 1:9; Philippians 3:13)

In meditating on the mountain climber's belt, I made some random observations that can be applied spiritually:

The higher one climbs, the greater the view, the farther the climber can see.

The higher one climbs, the closer he gets to the one waiting at the top.

The higher one climbs, the fewer the people with him. The valley is where the population is dense. Few people climb the high mountains, and fewer make it to the top.

To reach the pinnacle of God's will for your life may take you away from the crowd and bring you to a place where you can see things others can't. To get there, you'll have to keep your eyes on the Lord, who is, after all, the way and the truth and the life (John 14:6) and not be overly concerned with how many people are joining you in the climb. It may be just you and one other, but if that Other is Jesus, it doesn't have to be a lonely climb.

Jesus said, ". . . you will know the truth, and the truth will set you free." (John 8:32) Just as some see belts and their contents as restricting and burdensome, there are those that see God's truth as nothing but rules and limitations. But to those who know the Truth, it is the source of our weapons of war, our tools, our safety, and our connection with God, enabling us to go places we otherwise never could have imagined. It is what makes us *truly* free—free from Satan's lies and the consequences of believing them.

As you prepare for the day and any spiritual battles that it may bring, your prayer may sound something like this:

> "Lord, thank You for the belt of truth. As I put it on today, may it arm me for battle, equip me to do Your work without being overwhelmed, keep me close to You, preserve me through life's calamities, and enable me to scale the heights with You."

The Breastplate of Righteousness

. . . with the breastplate of righteousness in place . . .

Ephesians 6: 14

In battle it is vital to protect the heart. This is true both physically and spiritually. We are told to have the breastplate of righteousness in place (Ephesians 6:14) but anyone who attempts to accomplish that simply by trying harder to be more "righteous" knows what a losing battle that can be. God's Word says that "all our righteous acts are like filthy rags," (Isaiah 64:6) and rags offer pretty poor protection in battle.

It has been pointed out by those with superior background knowledge of biblical times that "filthy rags" refers to the rags women used during their monthly periods. I've heard teachers say the image was so we could see how "disgusting" our attempts at righteousness are to God. But I've come to believe that the prophet wasn't looking for an image that was merely disgusting. (I taught middle school for some years, and my students, especially the boys, could come up with much more disgusting things than that. Those guys were experts in "gross.")

These rags made a woman ceremonially "unclean" according to Jewish law, but so did touching a dead body or eating pork or any number of other things. Why would Isaiah choose this particular image as a picture of our "righteous acts?" Well, I have a theory.

In ancient times a woman's main purpose in life was to bear children. This was so important to the society that a woman who was unable to have children was considered "barren" and under a curse. For a woman facing that kind of stigma, the "filthy rags" were a painful monthly reminder that there was *no life* in her womb.

But suppose a single woman were to determine that she's going to create a baby out of her own sheer efforts. She fixes up a nursery in her house and furnishes it with a crib, a rocker, and a changing table. She buys diapers, baby clothes, and all the baby essentials. She memorizes What to Expect When You're Expecting and all of Dr. Dobson's books on childrearing. Finally, after nine months, she produces (*drum roll . . .*)

. . . filthy rags. Of course, with no husband involved, no life will be created.

Of course, this sounds ridiculous, but how many of us are doing this on a spiritual level?

We go to church—perfect attendance!—we give our tithe, we sing in the choir, we collect canned goods for the soup kitchen, and we make gallons of Kool-Aid for vacation Bible school. But our prayers remain lifeless, and we wonder why.

While there's nothing wrong with doing all these good things, the fact remains that without a relationship with our Bridegroom, there will be no life, just the spiritual equivalent to filthy rags.

I can't prove it, but I believe Isaiah chose an image that the people of his day would recognize as a picture of barrenness—not death, because where there's death there used to be life, but *barrenness*—where there was never life to begin with.

Our breastplate has to be *God's* righteousness, not ours, and the only way to protect our hearts is to give them over to Him.

Think of the ways our hearts are vulnerable. Our emotions try to rule us, rather than letting Christ reign. Our passions can take us in the wrong directions, and our desires can be for the wrong things. Our affections can go quickly from "things above" to things below. Even in wanting the right things, our motives can be wrong, and of course, there is the ever-present matter of attitude. Trying to manage all these things in our own strength is hopeless without God. The only thing to do is acknowledge our utter dependence on Him and ask Him to take over our hearts.

Putting on the "breastplate of righteousness" might sound something like this:

> "Lord, I give You my heart today. I choose You as my ruler, and I thank You that my emotions don't get to rule or define me. Lord, let my passion be for You, and as I delight myself in You, birth in me the same desires in my heart that You have for my life. Purify my motives, and give me a Christ-like attitude today. As I cast off the filthy rags of my own dead works and attempts at righteousness, I put on the breastplate of *Your* Righteousness."

The Readiness of the Gospel of Peace

> ". . . and your feet fitted with the readiness that comes from the gospel of peace."
>
> Ephesians 6:15

A soldier without adequate footwear can get into all kinds of trouble. His feet could slip, they could get injured, and even if the injuries didn't become fatally infected, which frequently occurred, they could slow the soldier down considerably, keeping him from getting to where he needed to be, even causing him to be captured by the enemy.

So how do we get "shod" for battle—how do we prepare? How do we "put on" the gospel of peace? By spending time focusing on the gospel—the "good news." To think about the things that stress us out only increases our anxiety; but meditating on the Truth of the gospel, *purposefully* focusing our attention on the Good News—that God loves us, that He is in control, that He has promised never to leave us, that He has died and we are forgiven, that we have heaven to look forward to—can settle our hearts and give us peace. How long should you spend in this kind of meditation on Scripture?

As long as it takes for the assurance of God's promises to give perfect peace—the peace God wants us to share with others.

How beautiful on the mountains
are the feet of those who bring good news,
who proclaim peace,
who bring good tidings,
who proclaim salvation,
who say to Zion, "Your God reigns!"
Isaiah 52:7

When we are "shod" with the gospel of peace, we can go and share the good news of God's love without being tripped up by the accuser (Satan), who may try to hinder us by reminding us of sins in our past that Christ has already paid for. With the peace of the gospel in us, we can ignore the enemy and continue to go wherever Jesus sends us.

If the enemy's accusations are starting to get to you, it's time to get back into God's Word and remind your heart that Satan is the father of lies, and that the God Who loves you is true, *however* you feel. (I'm not saying this is easy!)

As you get suited up for whatever the day may bring, you can pray something like this:

"Father, thank You for the gospel—the good news that Your Son Jesus died for my sins. I thank You for the peace of being forgiven. Let my feet be fitted with the readiness of the gospel of peace, that I may go and share that peace wherever You send me."

The Shield of Faith

In addition to all this, take up the shield of faith, with which you can extinguish all the flaming arrows of the evil one.
Ephesians 6:16

A soldier's shield was the most flexible part of his protective armor, able to be moved to deflect the enemy's arrows coming from multiple directions.

Satan can attack from all directions, too. He can attack our possessions, our health, our relationships, our families, our ministries, our confidence—or seemingly everything at once. Wherever those arrows are coming from, whatever they're attacking, the proper way to respond is with faith. And as we saw in the ice illustration, the important thing isn't how much faith one can muster up, but having that faith in the right place—or in the right Person. There is a great deal more that could and should be said about faith, some of which was covered in Chapter Six.

While the New Testament refers to the shield of (our) faith, the Old Testament refers to God's faithfulness. So this shield in a sense has two "layers"—faithfulness provided by God and the faith that is our response to it. The two together form an impenetrable barrier against the enemy.

"Taking up the shield of faith" may sound something like this:

> "Lord, thank You for the shield of faith. As I take it up today,
> I trust You to protect me from every arrow of the evil one:
> the big arrows and the little darts; the arrows I expect and
> see coming and the ones that seem to come out of nowhere;
> the ones aimed at me and the ones aimed at my loved ones.
> I trust You with all of it, Lord, and I thank You."

The Helmet of Salvation

Take the helmet of salvation . . .

Ephesians 6: 17

As we also discussed in Chapter Six, the battle over our souls is largely waged in the mind. (Remember the plastic snake in the garden?) It is in the mind that the devil wreaks havoc with his lies.

So why do we fall victim to Satan's lies? Shouldn't we know better than to listen to the devil? I think the answer to that is that most of us don't recognize the enemy of our souls. Forget the cartoonist's idea of this guy with red underwear and a pitchfork. The real devil, the enemy of our souls, is invisible. We can't see him, but **we can hear him**, because he speaks to us in our minds.—*Seriously?* Yes. I can't tell you what he looks like, but I can tell you exactly what he sounds like. (Are you ready for this?)

He sounds just like you.

(And when he's speaking to *me*, his voice sounds just like *mine*.)

He also speaks in the first person. It's not like that cartoon you've seen where the little angel sits on one shoulder telling you to do the right thing, and the little red imp sits on the other shoulder telling you to do the wrong thing. The devil isn't some creature who sits on your shoulder and says something like, "You should get drunk!" He knows you wouldn't fall for that.

The real devil gets into your mind and says, "*I'm* really stressed. *I* really need a drink. It will calm *my* nerves." And because he's speaking in the first person, and because he sounds just like you, you think that's your thought!

Then, after you've followed that thought with action, that same voice starts to heap on the guilt—for doing what he suggested in the first place! (By the way, he's also known as "the accuser."—Revelation 12:10) And again it sounds just like you, speaking in the first person. ("*I* can't believe *I* did that again! What's wrong with *me*?")

When God was delivering me from an eating disorder, I began to recognize those thoughts that sounded like me—like "I'll just eat a little, to hold me over until dinner .." and, "Maybe just one more." then, "Well, I've already blown it, I may as well finish the thing . . ." and finally, "I can't believe I ate that whole thing. I'm such an idiot!" followed by guilt, self-condemnation, and depression . . . which I would treat with more food . . .

OK, that's the bad news, and maybe you've had that kind of experience. But the good news is, God is battling for our minds, too! The difference is, *He's* not deceptive about it. He's given us the *Truth*—as in "You will know the truth, and the truth will set you free." We can know the Truth by reading God's Word—the Bible—and setting our minds on it.

What I didn't realize as a bulimic teenager was that my problem was not on my plate, it was in my mind. After about twelve years of slavery to food, as the truth about spiritual warfare became evident, I changed my focus from "my problem" to God's solutions. I set my mind on God's Word, filling my mind with its truth. For me, this meant spending my time reading the Bible, listening to the tapes friends were giving me, praying, journaling, going to Bible studies, singing praises to God, even telling my unsaved friends about Him. When you add that to the time I was taking care of my husband, two small children and the house, I didn't have *time* to feel sorry for myself or eat half the food in the refrigerator. As I took God's truth to heart, as I studied it and applied it to myself, as I made choices where I *purposefully* took God at His Word—*no matter how I felt*—I gradually grew to accept my status as God's child—loved, accepted, forgiven, and victorious. In other words, as I gave my *mind* to God, I was set free.

(Now I realize some of you will say I'm recommending a lifestyle that defines a person as a religious fanatic. All I know is, I'm happy, and the life I'm living now sure beats 12 years with my head in the toilet.)

I can't think of a better passage of Scripture when it comes to the importance of our minds than Romans 8. In fact, this is my favorite chapter of the New Testament, and if I were your counselor, I'd tell you to memorize it.

> Therefore, there is now *no condemnation* for those who are in Christ Jesus, because through Christ Jesus the law of the Spirit of life *set me free* from the law of sin and death. For what the law was powerless to do in that it was weakened by the sinful nature, God did by sending His own Son in the likeness of sinful man to be a sin offering. And so He condemned sin in sinful man, in order that the righteous requirements of the law might be fully met in us, who do not live according to the sinful nature, but according to the spirit." [italics mine]
>
> Romans 8:1–4

Today we have the term "mind set," and this is where you can win the battle. It's where you set your mind—again, it's a choice. Look at the next part of this passage, and notice how many times you see the word "mind:"

> Those who live according to the sinful nature have their minds set on what that nature desires; but those who live in accordance with the

> spirit have their minds set on what the spirit desires. The mind of sinful man is death, but the mind controlled by the spirit is life and peace; the sinful mind is hostile to God. It does not submit to God's law, nor can it do so. Those controlled by the sinful nature cannot please God.
>
> Romans 8: 5–8

So set your mind today on what God says. Ask Him to help you set your mind on the things *He* wants you thinking about. (There's a good list in Philippians 4:8 that you can use as a guideline.) And put on the helmet of salvation. It's the best protection from that pesky little voice that lies to you in the first person and sounds just like you.

And stop focusing on your problem. Your problem is not the problem! Keep your eyes on the Lord. I like the picture of a helmet that shows little side blinders to protect the eyes. With that picture in mind, I pray something like this:

> "Lord, I give You my mind today, taking every thought captive to make it obedient to Christ. I give You my thoughts, my ideas, my imagination, my creativity, my memories, my dreams, and my priorities. Cleanse them and make them what You want them to be. Fill my mind with Your Holy Spirit, infused with the personality You want me to have, and cover it with the helmet of Your salvation. Give me Your perspective, and help me to keep my focus straight ahead on You and whatever Your plan is for me today, not being distracted by the other things going on around me that try to steal my attention."

The Sword of the Spirit

> ". . . and the sword of the Spirit, which is the word of God."
>
> Ephesians 6: 17

So far we've been "putting on the whole armor of God." With the belt of truth, the breastplate of righteousness, the combat boots of the readiness of the gospel of peace, the shield of faith, and the helmet of salvation, we are well protected. But we are not here just to keep ourselves safe. A soldier's job is to "fight the good fight," and we have been given the "sword of the Spirit," the Word of God. As I described to you, God's Word brought healing to my mind and deliverance from an eating disorder. But the Word is also our offensive weapon to use against the enemy to combat his lies. During Jesus' temptation in the wilderness—and make no mistake about it, temptation is an attack!—He fought back with the Word of God.

> Then Jesus was led by the Spirit into the desert to be tempted by the devil. After fasting forty days and forty nights, he was hungry.
>
> The tempter came to him and said, "If you are the Son of God, tell these stones to become bread."
>
> Jesus answered, "It is written: 'Man does not live on bread alone, but on every word that comes from the mouth of God.'"
>
> Then the devil took him to the holy city and had him stand on the highest point of the temple. "If you are the Son of God," he said, "throw yourself down. For it is written:
>
> "'He will command his angels concerning you, and they will lift you up in their hands so that you will not strike your foot against a stone.'"
>
> Jesus answered him, "It is also written: 'Do not put the Lord your God to the test.'"
>
> Again, the devil took him to a very high mountain and showed him all the kingdoms of the world and their splendor "All this I will give you," he said, "if you will bow down and worship me."
>
> Jesus said to him, "Away from me, Satan! For it is written: 'Worship the Lord your God and serve him only.'"

> Then the devil left him, and angels came and attended him.
>
> Matthew 4: 1–11

James wrote, ". . . Resist the devil, and he will flee from you." (James 4: 7) As the Lord Jesus showed us, the way to resist the father of lies is with the truth of God's Word. Jesus had the Word hidden in His heart and had it ready to pull out any time it was needed.

Notice in this passage Satan also quoted Scripture. Not everyone who quotes the Bible is necessarily on the right side. Satan was quoting Psalm 91: 11 and 12, but he was leaving out part of it. Verse 11 says, "He will command his angels concerning you *to guard you in all your ways.*" [italics mine] In other words, God watches over His children as they innocently go about their day. This is *not* an invitation to jump off high towers and wait for the angels to catch us. Faith is not a circus performance. This is why it is important not only to know the words of Scripture, but to study them *in context.* Many cults have led gullible people astray by quoting Scripture wrongly, incompletely, or out of context. Instead of merely memorizing random single verses, it's good to memorize whole passages, or at least know the context of the verses you're memorizing. Then when you encounter doubts, fear, depression, condemnation (not to be confused with conviction over un-confessed sin), or any other assault from the enemy, these words can be your sword to defeat him.

What Armor Won't Do

Armor, even the Armor of God, doesn't prevent battles, it protects the soldier *in* the battle.The belt of truth doesn't keep battles and collisions from happening to us, but when they do happen, we'll have the weapons we need to fight the enemy's lies, and we'll be kept safe when we find ourselves in a collision of personalities and worldviews. This belt doesn't get us out of working, but with it we'll have every tool we need to get the job done. It won't keep life from seeming overwhelming at times, but it will keep us afloat. It won't give us a free ride up the mountain or keep us from stumbling along the way, but the truth (example: I John 1:9) will keep us from falling all the way down the mountain and having to start over from the bottom. When connected to Jesus, we can simply get back up where we stumbled and keep going.

In a similar way, the breastplate of righteousness doesn't keep us from being attacked—we will be, and we'll sometimes get knocked down. But the enemy will not be able to *penetrate* our hearts if they're covered with God's righteousness.

Having our feet fitted with the readiness that comes from the gospel of peace doesn't mean we can put our feet up and relax now! On the contrary, it enables us to go anywhere God wants to send us.

The shield of faith doesn't keep the fiery arrows of the evil one from coming at us, but it does extinguish them, *if* we're holding onto our faith and His faithfulness.

Having the helmet of salvation doesn't mean the enemy won't assault our minds from time to time, but God will provide the wisdom and discernment we need to sort out the truth. With our minds set on God and His Word, we'll recognize the lies for what they are, and they'll bounce off.

The sword of the Spirit, the Word of God, isn't just something we read every day "for luck." ("A chapter a day keeps the devil away"?) Jesus used the Word to resist the devil (Matthew 4:1–11), and if He needed it, we'd better believe we're going to need it, too! The Word of God should be something we live and breathe, not just read and talk about occasionally.

So while apparently battles are unavoidable, we can be encouraged that God is on our side. We just need to be on His, and make sure we have our armor in place and know how to wield the sword.

Victory!

Remember, you are a soldier in the greatest army on earth! It is also the most diverse. God's army is made up of men, women, and children; elderly, youthful, rich, poor, educated, unschooled, famous, obscure, bright, simple, weak, strong, disabled, healthy, terminally ill, loved, hated, free, and imprisoned. They have lived in virtually every populated corner of the globe over the past twenty centuries, speaking hundreds of languages, and having billions of different personalities and combinations of gifts.

Most importantly, this army is the one that wins in the end. Jesus said, ". . . on this rock I will build my church, and the gates Hades not overcome it." (Matthew 16:18b) Notice He said, "gates." We're not just defending ourselves from Satan's attacks, we're storming the gates of the enemy and rescuing those who have been imprisoned by his schemes and lies for too long.

If your prayers have been delayed and you have done all you know to do in obedience to God's Word, it could be that your prayers are more important than you realize, and there are "spiritual forces of evil in the heavenly realms" that are determined to stop you. All I can tell you is, be *more* determined. Keep fighting. You are not alone, and in the end, in ways we don't yet know, we *will* win.

Chapter Fourteen

BARRIER #14

SUPERSTITION

"Keep on, then, with your magic spells
and with your many sorceries,
which you have labored at since childhood.
Perhaps you will succeed,
perhaps you will cause terror.
All the counsel you have received has only worn you out!
Let your astrologers come forward,
those stargazers who make predictions
month by month,
let them save you from what is coming upon you.
Surely they are like stubble;
the fire will burn them up.
They cannot even save themselves
from the power of the flame.
Here are no coals to warm anyone;
here is no fire to sit by.
That is all they can do for you—
those you have labored with
and trafficked with since childhood.
Each of them goes on in his error;
there is not one that can save you."

Isaiah 47: 12–15

Anyone who thinks God incapable of sarcasm apparently has never read this passage in Isaiah. God was obviously very, very upset with His people. He had good reason.

These were the people whose predecessors He brought out of Egypt through numerous miracles, and for whom He opened up the Red Sea, then letting the waters close back in to destroy their enemies.

This was the nation He led through the wilderness, sustaining them with manna from heaven, flocks of quail, and water from the rock, and guiding them with a cloud by day and a pillar of fire by night. He saw to it that their clothes and shoes never wore out in the forty years they were in the wilderness. He opened up the Jordan River, collapsed the walls of Jericho, gave them victory over their enemies, and established them as a nation.

That nation had been slipping away from Him over the generations, taking His love for granted or forgetting Him entirely and going their own way. God's people were even turning to other gods, to magic, sorcery, astrology, and every other abominable practice their pagan neighbors had engaged in, things He had *specifically warned them* to have nothing to do with.

To read the history of the children of Israel, it's easy to see their foolishness—much easier than it was for them to see it themselves over the generations that it took to backslide that far. It would also be easy for us to believe that we would never be that foolish, especially if we had experienced all the miracles the LORD had done for His people.

Careful. "I would *never* do that!" has been famous last words often enough to merit some self-examination on our part.

First of all, I should point out that God has actually done much *more* for us even than He did for Israel. Even after the conquest of the Promised Land the children of Israel still had to make sacrifices to atone for their sins. And since people sin daily, their sacrifices never fully paid for their total forgiveness.

But just think—God loved us so much that He sent His own Son to *be* our sacrifice! Jesus, Who could have done the easy thing and stayed in heaven enjoying its glory, instead willingly came to this fallen planet, lived among sinful people, endured betrayal and hatred, and died on a cross—the most painful, degrading death. And why would He go through all this? To pay for a relationship with us—the ones He created, the ones who rejected Him. Not only has He taken care of us physically, as He did the children of Israel in Old Testament times, but He has paid the price for us to live *eternal* life in heaven—a life we certainly don't deserve and never, ever could have earned on our own.

Stop and think about how truly awesome such a gift is, how much we owe Him.

As foolish as the ancient Israelites were, would we not be even more foolish to turn our backs on our God and put our trust in anything or anyone else?

Now I know that in twenty-first-century America one doesn't see much idol worship in the forms that occurred in biblical times. Most of our cities don't have pagan temples complete with temple prostitutes and altars where human sacrifices and other abominations take place. Most of us don't have pagan altars or idols in our homes—that we know of! There are modern-day equivalents to these things in other countries and to a lesser extent in ours—Ouija boards, tarot cards, astrology, and the like. I don't know too many Christians who read their daily horoscopes or consult fortune tellers—although if you do, you should seriously re-examine your relationship with the One you claim you trust.

I really shouldn't have to mention this, but having seen an astrological chart posted in a church, I think I should add that you may also need to reexamine what your church teaches about such things.

Other superstitions exist in our society which are well known but are scarcely taken seriously. I knew a woman who would always feel a need to leave a place through the same door she entered through, and a man who if he spilled the salt had to throw a few grains of it over his left shoulder. You may know someone who avoids stepping on cracks in the sidewalk, is afraid of bad luck if she breaks a mirror (other than the mess, financial loss, and risk of being cut), and other "good luck" or "bad luck" concepts. Personally, my only belief on that subject is that it's "bad luck" to be superstitious.

While we scoff at these old superstitions, some of them have their roots in Christian traditions. I've read, for example, that Friday the 13th gained its bad reputation because Jesus was crucified on a Friday, and He and His disciples (including Judas) totaled 13 people. "Knocking on wood," according to some sources, had something to do with the Cross . . .

I'm not including this chapter because I think the reader is running around with horseshoes and rabbits' feet, looking for four-leaf clovers. In fact, I had *thought* I had nearly covered all the bases when it came to hindrances to prayer when I began taking more notice of things in my own Christian circles that have the appearance of new superstitions in the making.

"Christian Superstition?"

Anyone who has email or Facebook has probably received one of these: a prayer, beautifully written that may express exactly what you are praying for your friends and family. You get to the end, deciding it might be nice to pass it on to your loved ones, and you're about to do just that. But then you see it: a promise that if you pass this on to [a random number of] people within [an arbitrary amount of time] your prayers will all be answered. However, if you delete the prayer, something bad will happen to you.

Really?

How did such nonsense get mixed up with what otherwise seems to be a reasonable view of prayers and the God who answers them? What really disturbs me is the number of otherwise reasonable Christians I know who pass these on, complete with the bribes and threats. I have the distinct feeling that superstition has crept in to pollute our faith.

I could give numerous examples such as the one just mentioned, but they could take more time and attention than they deserve. Instead, I want to share what I consider the most appalling example that came to my attention lately. I would not have taken it seriously if I had not seen the multitude of responses on the website that convinced me there are some seriously deluded people out there.

How to Sell Your House and Your Soul

There is a certain website that tells its readers how to expedite the sale of a house, using occult methods under the guise of Christianity. First, the one who wants to sell his/her house is to purchase a statue of St. Joseph (Jesus' adoptive father), then bury it, facing the house, in the yard. Then the following "prayer" is suggested:

> **Prayer to Sell a House**
> O, Saint Joseph, you who taught our Lord the carpenter's trade, and saw to it that he was always properly housed, hear my earnest plea. I want you to help me now as you helped your foster-child Jesus, and as you have helped many others in the matter of housing. I wish to sell this [house/property] quickly, easily, and profitably and I implore you to grant my wish by bringing me a good buyer, one who is eager, compliant, and honest, and by letting nothing impede the rapid conclusion of the sale.
>
> Dear Saint Joseph, I know you would do this for me out of the goodness of your heart and in your own good time, but my need is very great now and so I must make you hurry on my behalf.
>
> Saint Joseph, I am going to place you in a difficult position with your head in darkness and you will suffer as our Lord suffered, until this [house/property] is sold. Then, Saint Joseph, I swear before the cross and God Almighty, that I will redeem you and you will receive my gratitude and a place of honour in my home.
>
> Amen.
>
> *prayers-for-special-help.com/prayer-to-sell-house.html#sthash.KQ1dhXy2.dpuf*

Friends, this is wrong on so many levels I hardly know where to start.

Can we agree that one of the most basic tenets of our faith is the Ten Commandments? Praying to anyone besides God clearly breaks the very First Commandment. (Exodus 20:3)

Having a statue of anyone in heaven and talking to that statue—praying to that statue—is blatantly breaking the Second Commandment. (Exodus 20:4 & 5)

Besides breaking the first two of the Ten Commandments, God has repeatedly pointed out how illogical it is to attribute power to something man-made.

> "Some pour out gold from their bags
> and weigh out silver on the scales;
> they hire a goldsmith to make it into a god,
> and they bow down and worship it.
> They lift it to their shoulders and carry it;
> they set it up in its place, and there it stands.
> From that spot it cannot move.
> Though one cries out to it, it does not answer;
> it cannot save him from his troubles."
>
> Isaiah 46: 6 & 7

There are many, many other passages of scripture that point out the absurdity of looking to man-made objects for solutions to one's problems, but why is even one passage necessary? Are we really that gullible?

As if attributing supernatural power to an inanimate object weren't bad enough, the person wanting to sell a house is directed to *purchase* such an item. When Simon the sorcerer tried to buy the Holy Spirit from the apostles, "Peter answered: 'May your money perish with you, because you thought you could buy the gift of God with money!'" (Acts 8:20)

After purchasing the statue, the seller is instructed to bury it in the ground facing the house. Is this ritual ever mentioned in scripture? Who decided that this was the way to sell a house? As God is quoted by the prophet Isaiah,

> ". . . These people come near to me with their mouth
> and honor me with their lips,
> but their hearts are far from me.

Their worship of me
is made up of only rules taught by men."
(Isaiah 29:13)

This kind of random, specific instruction ("Buy a statue. Bury it in your yard, facing the house . . .") is the kind of activity practiced regularly by people involved in witchcraft and the occult. God has clearly commanded, "Do not practice divination or sorcery." (Leviticus 19:26)

Why would one consult St. Joseph rather than God? As scripture says, "Should not a people inquire of their God? Why consult the dead on behalf of the living?" (Isaiah 8:19)

Some will say, "But St. Joseph isn't dead! He's very much alive in heaven!" Yes, I agree, and please don't think I have any bad opinions about the man God chose to be Jesus' earthly dad. I am saying—and Joseph would agree with me—that this human being should never be put in the role of God Himself!

When Paul and Barnabas came to Lystra, God healed a crippled man through Paul. The people tried to worship the apostles and offer sacrifices to them. Rather than being pleased with the flattery, Paul and Barnabas were appalled.

> "But when the apostles Barnabas and Paul heard of this, they tore their clothes and rushed out into the crowd, shouting, "Men, why are you doing this? We too are only men, human like you."
>
> Acts 14: 14 & 15

Granted, there is one difference between this incident and the whole St. Joseph business. Paul and Barnabas were still in the flesh, and the man Joseph is in heaven now and like one of the angels. However, that still does not mean it's ever acceptable to worship or pray to him, or any other departed saint, for that matter. Even the angelic messenger of Revelation refused to receive worship.

> I, John, am the one who heard and saw these things. And when I had heard and seen them, I fell down to worship at the feet of the angel

> who had been showing them to me. But he said to me, "*Do not do it!* I am a fellow servant with you and with your brothers the prophets and of all who keep the words of this book. *Worship God!*" [italics mine]
>
> Revelation 22: 8 & 9

Yes, Joseph is in heaven, but don't think for a minute that he's pleased with the way his name and memory are being used in this kind of superstition.

Another appalling thing about this "prayer" is the pure selfishness it expresses, selfishness in the form of impatience, laziness, and greed.—"I wish to sell this [house/property] quickly, easily, and profitably"

Whatever happened to "Thy will be done"? The impatience is accentuated by the unwillingness to wait for the saint to grant the request "out of the goodness of your heart and in your own good time." Instead, the petitioner decides, "I must make you hurry on my behalf."

"Make"? Really? Who exactly has the power here? Who is it that knows best? If it is the person selling the house, why is he even praying at all? If he knows better and can make it happen, why involve an innocent saint in his nasty business?

Hang on, it gets worse.

So, since St. Joseph is apparently a little slow, now he needs to be *tortured* into submission—"you will suffer as our Lord suffered until this [house/property] is sold."

In other words, it's like stuffing a genie back into a bottle until he agrees to cooperate. When he gets uncomfortable enough, the wish will be granted.

And when the house does sell? "I swear before the cross and God Almighty that I will redeem you and you will receive my gratitude and a place of honour in my home."

Talk about a fair-weather friend! This bargaining mentality has no place in the Christian's prayer life. Either we love God and trust that He knows best and are willing to say "Thy will be done," or we don't. Even if this prayer were being offered to God, the attitude it reflects is the exact *opposite* of what God desires from us. Review the fruits of the Spirit in Galatians 5:22 and 23, and ask yourself if any of these attitudes are reflected in this "prayer."

"The LORD your God . . . shows no partiality and accepts no bribes." (Deuteronomy 10: 17) People, you can be sure that God cannot be manipulated! If He can't be bribed, He (and His saints) certainly can't be threatened! And I might add, anyone who has died in the LORD and gone to heaven will not be suffering anymore! (Would you really want anything else to be the case?)

There are a few more ways in which this whole ritual and prayer violate God's will for His children, His will as expressed in no less than Jesus' Sermon on the Mount:

It has the person swearing "by the cross and God Almighty," when Jesus clearly said, "But I tell you, Do not swear at all . . ." (Matthew 5: 34)

The purpose of this practice is clearly to achieve one's financial goal, specifically to sell one's house. Any such goal should be secondary for the Christian. As I hope you've seen by now, God's priority is for us to be conformed to the image of Christ, to know Him, to serve Him, and to experience the joy of relationship with Him. Jesus said,

> "No one can serve two masters. Either he will hate the one and love the other, or he will be devoted to the one and despise the other. You cannot serve both God and money."
>
> Matthew 6:24

It's pretty obvious which one is being served in this whole ritual.To the person who is thinking, "But I need to sell this house!" Jesus says:

> "For the pagans run after all these things, and *your heavenly Father knows that you need them.* But seek *first* his kingdom and his righteousness, and all these things will be given to you as well."
>
> Matthew 6: 32 & 33 (italics mine)

God certainly knows your needs. Again, do you trust Him or not? One might find examples of people who have cast the St. Joseph spell and had it work. I've heard that some people "swear by it." Besides what you already know Jesus said about swearing, one could reasonably ask,

"So what?" Just because my house sold quickly, does that have anything to do with what I did with my store-bought idol? If it did, I would say that the source was not God. Getting something—anything—from an unknown source sets me up to begin trusting that source, and if that source isn't the God who loves me, I could be getting into some dark places. (Yes, I mean the demonic.)

"What good will it be for a man if he gains the whole world, yet forfeits his soul?" (Matthew 16:26) There are plenty of financially prosperous people in this world who do not know God, and until and unless they do, their destiny is not an enviable one. Don't sell your soul that cheaply. I would rather die in the arms of Jesus than live as a billionaire in Satan's service.

So, ". . . choose for yourselves this day whom you will serve." (Joshua 24: 15) If it is God, then know His Word, live it, and make pleasing Him your ultimate goal. If your goal is anything else, then practice all the superstition you want. But please don't call yourself a Christian.

Chapter Fifteen

WHY THE DRY SPELLS?

"But when the sun came up, the plants were scorched, and they withered, because they had no root."
Mark 4: 6

For our first nine anniversaries my husband Marty didn't quite "get it" when it came to buying roses. He's the type of guy that thinks it's a waste of money to buy something that doesn't serve any practical purpose and that will be dead in a matter of days. He's got a point. Still, early in our marriage I dropped enough hints that on our tenth anniversary he gave me roses.

Boy, did he give me roses! I was given, not a bouquet of roses, but a rose *garden!* I can still recall watching out the kitchen window as Marty hauled away the scruffy bushes that had filled our circular driveway, hauled in railroad ties, arranged them, and filled them with several loads of dark brown topsoil. This was no small task, and as it started to rain and he continued to work, getting drenched in the process, I was especially touched by his dedication. (Once he gets his mind set on something . . . !) By the end of the day we had a two-tiered bed just waiting to be filled with something awesome.

Then came the fun part: going to the nursery and picking out rose bushes to plant. We selected about twenty of them, and no two were alike. They were a dazzling assortment of colors: red, white, pink, yellow, peach, lavender, reddish-orange, red-and-white, pink-and-yellow, even a rose that started out a bright reddish-orange bud and turned various colors as it opened, ending with a smoky purplish-red. They also came in various sizes, shapes from ruffled to urn-shaped, and fragrances ranging from spicy to fruity. They had wonderful names like "Tiffany," "Angel Face," "Lincoln," and "Smoky" (the one with ever-changing colors).

I was delighted with my anniversary present.

Once they were planted and fertilized, I dutifully watered them every day. Over the summer I watched them explode into a panorama of color, which I cut and shared with friends, neighbors, and patients at the hospital where I volunteered. I knew each rose by name and could even identify some of them just by their fragrance. As the summer drew to a close, I took some of my best blooms to the county fair and came home with multiple ribbons, most of them blue. I was confident that I was quite the expert rose gardener indeed!

My confidence was shattered, however, when that winter all my "babies" died!

Baffled, I went to the nursery to buy more bushes and expressed my dismay to the salesman. I explained to him how I had weeded them, pruned them, sprayed them, fertilized them, watered them every day . . .

"There's your problem," the salesman interrupted. "You're not supposed to water roses every day."

"I'm not?" I asked, suddenly feeling not so professional after all.

The expert explained that when the roses were watered just a little every day, their roots spread out just under the surface of the ground. Then when winter came and the top layer of soil froze, the roots froze with it and the roses died. However beautiful they were during the warm weather, because their roots were shallow, they couldn't survive the winter.

However, he explained, when roses are soaked heavily just once a week, the water sinks deep into the ground. Then when the weather gets hot and dry between waterings, the roses will stretch their roots down to where the water is. When winter comes and the top of the ground freezes, the roses' roots remain safe deep underground, ready to send up new shoots in the spring.

In other words, the dry spells are what help the roses survive the winters.

The application to our lives is probably obvious by now, but I'll state it anyway. If we were always given everything we wanted the moment we wanted it, if God spoon-fed us throughout our lives, if we never felt any need, we would be comfortable, contented, naïve, weak, spoiled, and useless. It's the "dry spells" that require us to stretch our faith to levels we have never reached before. Anyone can believe in God when prayers are answered instantly. (We would probably take Him for granted, as well, as we've seen.) But God is honored most when we trust Him during the hard times, especially when trusting Him is counterintuitive and deliberate. As Jesus pointed out in His parable of the sower and the seeds, the faith of many dies out when trials come, because their roots don't go deep enough to sustain them.(Mark 4: 16–17)

I can't overemphasize that prayer is *not* a means to get us things we want, when we want them. It is a way to draw close to God, to grow our trust in Him, and to become more like Him. When the dry spells come—and they will—we can let them discourage us, or we can use those times to exercise faith and become stronger. We can say, "God, I may not feel Your presence or see You working in my life right now, but I trust that You *are* working. I thank You that Your truth doesn't depend on my feelings or circumstances." We can *choose* to trust Him, let the roots of our faith go deep, and wait for the day our faith will blossom into something breathtakingly beautiful.

So in a way true prayer is the opposite of begging, claiming, or demanding something from God. True prayer is acknowledging His lordship over our lives, yielding to Him because He is all-knowing, all-powerful, and all-loving, and trusting that His will for us is better than anything we could imagine.

True prayer is surrender.

Some of us have a problem with the word "surrender." The reason is probably that we're thinking of the kind of surrender that happens on a battlefield, where a beaten, bloody, half-dead soldier has no choice but to give himself up to his enemy. But that is only one kind of surrender.

Would it help instead to think of the surrender that a bride gives her bridegroom on her wedding night? Depending on one's attitude, surrender can be an indescribably joyous act of the will, and the peace it brings is beyond anything the world or its treasures have to offer.

"Delight yourself in the LORD, and he will give you the desires of your heart." (Psalm 37:4) That is because when we delight in the Lord, what we desire is *more of Him,* and He is always willing to give us that!

Prayer isn't a skill we learn and then use for the rest of our lives to get what we want. Prayer is a journey with the God Who loved us enough to give His life up for us, and Who has promised never to leave us or forsake us. He is the One climbing with us to ever greater heights, encouraging us when we're afraid, challenging us when we're lazy, correcting us when we're going the wrong way, comforting us when we're sad, forgiving us when we've failed, picking us up when we fall, healing us when we're hurt, strengthening us when we're weak, reviving us when we're tired, providing for us when we're in need, protecting us when we're under attack, and most of all *loving* us, always and forever.

Enjoy the journey.

Epilogue

This morning Mr. Hollywood and I were doing our breakfast routine. I tossed a piece of food down the hall, and he ran after it with gusto. I threw another piece down the stairs; he dashed down to get it and came running back up. It was then that I noticed something different.

He was watching *me* this time!

He's finally learning.

And if he can learn, so can we.

Epilogue

Appendix I

Top Ten Ways to Guarantee Your Prayers Won't Get Answered (With Apologies to David Letterman)

(11. For husbands: Disrespect and mistreat your wife. (I Peter 3:7))

10. Give God tiny bits of your leftover time and second-rate resources, and reserve the best for other things. Squander your time, but hoard your stuff; don't tithe. (Malachi) Fill your day/mind with secular media nonstop, so God can't get a word in edgewise. (Romans 12:2)

9. Avoid that person you've been having a problem with, or who has a problem with you. (Matthew 5:23 & 24)

8. Accuse God of not understanding how important this is; He's just not as smart as you are. (Isaiah 55: 8 & 9) Believe that health and wealth are the most important things, and if you aren't healthy and wealthy, God must not care about you. (II Corinthians12:7–10)

7. Ask once. Then if nothing happens right away, give up. Say, "See? I knew it wouldn't work." (Luke 18:1)

6. After saying "Amen," immediately tell yourself all the reasons God's probably not going to answer. For extra assurance, tell others, too. (James 1:6 & 7)

5. Keep God confined to one small area in your life, away from all the everyday events and *far* from any guilty pleasures, bad habits, and secret sins; He wouldn't want to be around all that stuff, anyway. (Psalm 66:18)

4. Make a list of all the bad things that have been done to you, and who did it. Memorize it and recite it often. Share it with others and invite them to be offended with you. (Mark 11: 24 & 25)

3. Ignore what God has done for you in the past, or complain about the way He did it or about what He hasn't done. Whatever you do, don't be grateful! (Philippians 4:6)

2. Ask not what you can do for God; ask what He can do for you. (James 4:3)

AND...the Number One way to make sure your prayers don't get answered:

1. Don't pray. (James 4:2)

Appendix II

The Warrior's Prayer (for the War on Terror)

Father in Heaven, we come to You acknowledging our utter dependence upon you.

Today we have enemies we can't see, but You have given us friends we can't see, and You see everything.

Our enemies have plans we don't know about, but so do You, and You know everything.

They have done things we couldn't stop, but You can do anything, and no one can stop You.

All-seeing, all-knowing, all-powerful God, we pray that no one on this planet would be harmed by a terrorist attack today.

We pray for any misguided souls scheduled to be suicide bombers this day. Plant enough doubt in their minds to make them hesitant and enough fear in their hearts to change their minds. Reveal to them a way of escape, and give them the courage and the opportunity to take it. Send them someone or something to present the truth of the gospel to them. Open their minds to understand it, and open their hearts to believe it, that they may renounce their hatred, embrace Your mercy, and receive salvation. May they be transformed into powerful, effective, passionate, joyful, fearless witnesses for You. Use them to light up the darkest corners of the world and of the hearts of men as they preach the gospel, plant churches, and ignite revival wherever they go.

Lord, as for those whose hearts are hardened and whose minds are still set on evil, we pray that today their communications will fail, their computers will crash, their data will get deleted, their cell phones will disconnect, and their transportation will break down; may their calculations be wrong, their timing be off, their weapons malfunction, and their bombs fail to detonate. Throw the enemy's camp into confusion, and thwart every plan they have, especially those scheduled to be carried out today. And when everything they try has failed, help them to see that it's because they have been serving the wrong god, that they may know that You are the true and living God, and that even then some of them might believe in You and be saved.

As for those who will never repent (for You know the end from the beginning) we pray that You would remove them from this world before they have a chance to drag anyone else down to hell with them. We pray for the children who are in terrorist training camps; Lord, shield their minds from whatever brainwashing they're being subjected to, and instead, give every one of them visions and dreams of You, that they may know that You are real, that You are there, and that You love them. Help them get to a place that is safe and where they will be loved and given an opportunity to know Christ.

We pray for anyone, anywhere on the planet who is a target of terrorists, especially those who are not yet ready for eternity. Shield them and spare their lives. Help them and those who have already survived terrorist attacks to know that You are giving them another chance to know You. Help them to seize that opportunity, seek You, and find You, that they may commit the rest of their lives to trusting, serving, and honoring You.

We pray for those who are in positions of authority—princes, presidents, and prime ministers. Give them the wisdom, the willingness, and the courage to do Your will. May anyone who is willfully defying You be removed from office and replaced by another who will seek You and do Your will.

We lift up those whose job it is to discern the identities and locations of terrorists: the Secret Service, the FBI, the CIA, and Homeland Security. We lift up all those serving in the Army, the Navy, the Air Force, the Marines, the Coast Guard, the Reserves, the National Guard, the Border Patrol, TSA and all security personnel, as well as the police and all law enforcement agencies. We pray also for all of their legitimate counterparts worldwide. If any terrorists have infiltrated their ranks, may they be apprehended and rendered harmless, even turned into allies. May each of the others be in the right place at the right time; may they see what they need to see, hear what they need to hear, understand what they need to understand, and do what they need to do. Give them discernment beyond their human abilities, and give them supernatural boldness and protection as they confront evil. We pray also for any civilians who are being called to take part in the War on Terror; may they have the wisdom, the courage, and the dedication they need to fulfill their calling, whatever it may be.

And may we all be diligent in prayer, knowing that ultimately we depend on You for our safety and our lives.

In Jesus' precious Name, Amen

Notes

TITLE PAGE

"Praise You in This Storm," Casting Crowns
From album "Lifesong," 2005
Writers: Bernie Herms, John Mark Hall
Published by Sony/ATV Tree Publishing, Word Music LLC, Warner/Chappell Music, Inc.

CHAPTER TWO

"City Slickers," 1991 Metro-Goldwyn Mayer Studios Inc.
Writers: Lowell Ganz, Babaloo Mandel
Director: Ron Underwood

"All I Ask of You," from "Phantom of the Opera"
Written by Andrew Lloyd Webber/Richard Stilgoe/Charles Hart
Scheffel Music Corp., The Really Useful Group Ltd.

CHAPTER THREE

"A Knight's Tale," 2001 Columbia Pictures Inc.
Writer and Director: Brian Helgeland

CHAPTER FOUR

Naghmeh Abedini, speech at Liberty University
September 17, 2013

CHAPTER FIVE

But God . . . by Nancy Sheldon, 2013

CHAPTER SEVEN

"Moses" TNT 1995
Produced by Lorenzo Minoli

CHAPTER TEN

Catching Fire, from *the Hunger Games* trilogy by Suzanne Collins
New York, Scholastic Press 2009

CHAPTER ELEVEN

The Hiding Place by Corrie Ten Boom
1971 Chosen Books

CHAPTER FOURTEEN

prayers-for-special-help.com/prayer-to-sell-house.html#sthash.KQ1dhXy2.dpuf

CPSIA information can be obtained
at www.ICGtesting.com
Printed in the USA
SHW022204150919
2042FS

9 781609 201067